MINISTRY
on
FIRE

Glen & Lisa,

Blessings abound
to God's people. You are
growing in joy with us all.

Enjoying Jesus' smile,

Bruce

MINISTRY *on* FIRE

Fanning the Flame
of Your Congregation

B. BRUCE HUMPHREY

CHALICE
PRESS

ST. LOUIS, MISSOURI

Cover art: Digital Stock
Cover and interior design: Elizabeth Wright

Visit Chalice Press on the World Wide Web at
www.chalicepress.com

10 9 8 7 6 5 4 3 2 1   05 06 07 08 09 10

Library of Congress Cataloging–in–Publication Data

Humphrey, B. Bruce.
   Ministry on fire : fanning the flame of your congregation / B. Bruce Humphrey.
      p. cm.
   Includes bibliographical references.
   ISBN-10: 0-827223-30-7 (pbk. : alk. paper)
   ISBN-13: 978-0-827223-30-1
   1. Church renewal–Biblical teaching. 2. Revivals. 3. Bible–Criticism, interpretation, etc. I. Title.
   BS680.C48H86 2005
   269–dc22

                                                            2005013304

Printed in the United States of America

Contents

Foreword

When I was a youngster playing basketball, I became fascinated by the concept of momentum. At one point a team seemed to be controlling the game, then all of a sudden something would happen. The momentum would switch, and the other team would take control of the game.

I'll never forget my senior year in high school. We had lost two of our first three games. Our coach decided that the way to turn the season around was to become a running, fast-breaking team. Even though I was cocaptain, he sat me on the bench because I was not known for my speed. In the fourth game we were playing our archrival, White Plains, the team favored to win the league. In the middle of the third quarter they were leading by fourteen points, and it looked to be a sad day in Mudville. Thinking the game was over, the coach looked down the bench and said, "Kenny, get in the game."

The first five times down the court I drove to the left corner and let fly long jump shots that hit nothing but net–five times in a row. In a short period of time, the whole momentum of the game changed, and we eventually won in sudden-death overtime. The momentum changed not only for that game but for the rest of the season as well, and we went on to win the league.

That dramatic moment during my high school basketball season has fascinated me all through my life. Therefore, I was thrilled when our pastor, Bruce Humphrey, decided to write a book on momentum. I was excited to read his insights, not only because Bruce is one of the brightest, most thoughtful people I know but also because I have seen momentum in action ever since he took over our church. When he arrived a number of years ago, the average age in our congregation was sixty-two, and attendance was heading downward. Bruce immediately created positive energy. He took his staff and lay leaders away to set a vision for the church that would inspire their hearts and souls. What was the result? Today, at the beginning of every service, the officiating pastor stands up and says, "We believe close encounters with Jesus of Nazareth transform lives. Our mission is to make Jesus smile." Turning the church over to Jesus and making him central to our church life has changed the momentum. Now we are one of the fastest growing churches in our area. So Bruce Humphrey knows about momentum from a personal standpoint. After studying momentum, he is ready to share his insights to help churches all over the country come alive and head in a direction that makes a positive difference.

This book is focused on pastors and churches, but the concepts apply in every organization, whether you're talking about a family, a business, or a volunteer operation. Read *Ministry On Fire* and get on fire for your life and your organization! Thanks, Bruce, for being our momentum guide.

Ken Blanchard
Coauthor of *The One Minute Manager*® and *The Servant Leader*
and cofounder of the Center for Faithwalk Leadership

Acknowledgments

I want to thank those whose collaboration turned this writing project into a wonderful experience. First, thank you to Ken Blanchard who saw the potential for this as a Christian leadership book and gave me opportunities to test out some of the material in presentations to his leadership groups. He enthusiastically supported the idea of this book and cheered me on. Also, thanks to those who read early drafts of this material and found ways to balance helpful suggestions with enough encouragement to keep me going—Angela and Ellie from our staff, and fellow pastors and covenant partners Alan, Mark, and Robbie. Huge thanks to three writers who meticulously edited and improved the manuscript: our son Justus, and good friends Bob and Jeannette. Thanks to Gay for discovering our "out-of-the-box" mainline congregation and recommending this manuscript to her husband Russ so that an "out-of-the-box" denominational pastor could work with an "out-of-the-box" denominational publisher. My condolences and thanks go to the family of my editor, Jane McAvoy. Jane worked with me in a caring, professional manner, but then died days before this manuscript was finished.

I could not have completed this task without the love and support of the staff and leadership of Rancho Bernardo Community Presbyterian Church. The Thursday morning men's covenant group—Allan, Ed, and Sheldon—has provided constant vigilance to keep me faithful to my calling. The Thursday evening covenant group was constant in their prayers and encouragement when I wavered and almost lost my momentum for this book. Speaking of prayer support, I need to thank the monthly nondenominational pastor's prayer group that not only listened to some of my ideas about leadership, but prayed devotedly for this project for more than two years.

So many people have helped me learn and refine these lessons, but I particularly appreciate those who watched me test these ideas and encouraged my growth as a leader in our ministries in Alaska and Arizona. I appreciate the loving support of our children who grew up experimenting with many of these life principles and proved they work outside the church as well. Thanks to my extended family for being proud of my success.

My best friend and the most important person in my life is my wife. She has heard this material talked through on long hikes, extended vacations, and too many days off. She has helped me tweak and refine my thinking as I played with why momentum works the way it does. She was my writing tutor back in graduate school when I couldn't put sentences into a paragraph and has believed not only in my writing but also in this book for pastors and church leaders, even when I doubted. She has persisted with me from conception of the ideas through the birth pangs of delivering the manuscript to the publisher. Kathy, I love you.

Bruce
San Diego

INTRODUCTION

Momentum as a Spiritual Force

Most church members want to see their churches enjoy strong growth, both spiritual and numerical. Most church members hope their church is known in the community as a positive force for good. Most church members desire deeper commitment among fellow members. Of course, most church leaders want all these same things. However, few church leaders know how to help it happen.

Instead of consistent growth, the majority of churches in America struggle to maintain their current levels of commitment and size. When at least seventy-five percent of churches in America are either at a plateau or dwindling in membership, the leaders of these churches have two choices. Either they can defend their dwindling membership as the price of being the faithful remnant, or they can decide to change direction to grow intentionally both spiritually and numerically. Unfortunately, too many church leaders have chosen the first option. I want to convince fellow church leaders to choose growth.

The Missing Ingredient: Momentum

I believe many churches are perched on the edge of exciting renewal. I also believe that God desires followers of Jesus to experience an awakening that would fill the churches with excitement and joy. I believe the Holy Spirit awaits the opportunity to release this awakening across our land. Unfortunately, few churches are currently experiencing the kind of growth in depth of faith and numbers that is possible in our spiritually hungry nation. Why are so few churches experiencing awakening? Why do most churches struggle in survival mode?

Let's quit blaming the preaching. (Yes, most of us who preach could spend more time working on our sermons. But this is not the essential problem.) Let's quit blaming the music. Growing, enthusiastic churches have a wide variety of worship and musical styles. Let's stop blaming the average church member. Few church members join with the hope of remaining mediocre in their faith. Most church members are more than happy to support the direction set by the church leaders. (We will deal later with those few who vehemently oppose the changes needed to create a positive spiritual direction.) It is not a lack of prayer or some spiritual problem that keeps most churches stuck in the same old patterns. For the most part we have a *leadership problem*. Simply put, a key ingredient is being overlooked by most church leaders in their decision making. This ingredient is spiritual momentum.

Momentum comes to us from the realm of physics. Physicists have formulas that show how the movement of an object is related to its mass and velocity. In the physical universe we know, for instance, that it takes energy to break the inertia of an object to get it moving in a new direction. Once the object is moving in the new direction, however, its momentum keeps it going in that same direction.

Momentum is easier to understand in practical life than in physics formulas. Years ago my wife made her first serious attempt at sports. A non-athlete through her life, in her early thirties she signed up for classes in racquetball so that we could play together. We began a weekly date of playing three games of racquetball with each other. Because I had been a high-school and college athlete, our early games included my jogging around the back of the court to get some aerobic exercise as well as playing the games. I served easy lobs for her to return. Along with our weekly dates, at the encouragement of her instructor, she joined a women's league and began to improve dramatically. Our games grew closer. We became much more even in our abilities. Occasionally she would beat me. Then it happened.

About six months into her lessons, at the encouragement of her instructor, Kathy signed up for a women's round-robin competition. This would initiate her into the realm of genuinely competitive sports. Her first games were against the former champion of the league.

Although the instructor and most of the rest of the women knew the champion's reputation, Kathy did not know who this person was. Kathy naïvely assumed she was pitted in the opening round against someone of equal abilities. Within the first two serves Kathy made a wonderful assumption: "Wow, my instructor must think I am better than I realized, because this lady is really good." This thought gave Kathy the energy to play beyond her former abilities. She got a couple of serves into the corner. She scored a few points. Then momentum took over. The other woman, frustrated that this new player was doing so well, began to miss even easy shots. In the momentum swing, while the former champion spiraled into negative momentum, Kathy could do nothing wrong. She was making kill shots and dominating the game. When Kathy came out of the court and gave the instructor the scores, the scorekeeper wrote them down in the wrong order, giving the victories to the other woman. Kathy corrected the scorekeeper, "No, I won." All the women grew strangely silent. It wasn't until she learned the other woman's reputation that Kathy realized why everyone was so astonished at her victory.

The Power of Momentum

Athletes and coaches know the power of momentum. A team with momentum on the court or the field is nearly unbeatable. Momentum is as important an ingredient as the natural talents and physical abilities of the athletes. Talented athletes who lose focus and begin to doubt their skills can quickly spiral into negative momentum. Less-skilled athletes who experience a taste of success and begin to believe in themselves can build and maintain the momentum to beat much more skilled opponents. Momentum is an important part of sports!

Momentum likewise influences the workplace. An unhappy, complaining colleague at work can create negative momentum. On the other hand, an employee who establishes a reputation as a hard worker in the organization often receives rewards because of the positive momentum. One of the primary tasks of managers is to generate positive momentum.

Momentum affects family relationships. The teenager who breaks a parent's trust quickly learns the power of negative expectations. The suspicious parent and frustrated teen can become caught in the trap of negative momentum. Unfaithfulness in a marriage can create not only broken trust but also negative momentum. When the momentum of love is wounded by unfaithfulness, distrust takes on a momentum of its own. Comments formerly seen as neutral become daggers in an atmosphere of distrust. Restoring positive momentum and healing trust can take years.

Students and teachers experience the incredible power of momentum. A student who writes a poor paper at the beginning of the semester creates low expectations on the part of the teacher. Once this is in place, the student must excel to build positive momentum. On the other hand, this same student can establish a reputation for good grades and excellence early in the academic year and ride the tide of momentum to scholarships and an outstanding higher education.

We live in a world in which momentum is incredibly powerful in our lives. God created us this way. Psychologists can describe it in terms of personal habits and patterns. Sociologists can study it under the category of culture. Historians research its effect in key political and military events. However, most of us as church leaders put little thought into the connection in the spiritual realm between personal revival, church renewal, national awakening, and the principle of momentum.

Momentum in a Church's Life

Might our churches be as influenced by momentum as other areas of society are? If our churches are affected by momentum, wouldn't it be worth taking this powerful force into consideration as we make important church decisions? Is there spiritual momentum as much as emotional and physical momentum? I believe so.

I first considered the power of momentum when I began my ministry in a small Indian fishing village on an island in Alaska. I discovered it through the daily discipline of building and maintaining the wood fire to heat our home. It took me several years to make the connection between what I learned from fire building in Alaska to the way we make decisions as church leaders.

I recall a popular Christian campfire song from the 1970s that suggested a spark was sufficient to start a fire. I sang this popular song often in youth services through much of the 1980s. I enjoy the imagery of God's love being like a warm fire. The image is cozy and comforting. The song has just one problem. Whoever penned the words never tried to make a fire from green wood in a wet snowstorm in Alaska. I have. Believe me, in such conditions it takes a lot more than a spark to get the fire going!

Our first year in a native fishing village in Alaska taught us that heat is very precious. The primary source of heat for our church-owned home was a wood stove in the living room. Arriving from

Arizona in late November, we discovered that the woodpile consisted mostly of fresh-cut, donated, unseasoned logs. We quickly learned what it takes to start a fire and keep it going. Our second son was born in January in the kitchen. Why in the kitchen? I had not yet learned how to maintain a wood fire to heat the entire house. Because the rest of the house was too cold, we opened the oven door and heated the kitchen to an acceptable temperature for delivery of a baby.

That first winter in Alaska our older son learned to pray, "Please, God, help us keep the fire going so the house will be warm." Over those few months we learned some important lessons about building and maintaining fires. Unseasoned wood sputters more than burns. Too much paper without enough kindling does not make a lasting fire. In fact, too much paper can create an unwanted chimney fire. Chimney fires can threaten to burn the house down.

By the end of our first winter we had learned to chop the wood into smaller sizes to provide more burning surfaces. We learned to control the airflow into the wood stove so that more of the heat radiated into the room and less went up the chimney. We learned that kindling is crucial to re-ignite the fire when it has gone out during the night. Eventually, we learned how to bank the fire for the night so that the coals remained hot all night. We learned to dry the wet wood for several hours before putting it directly into the wood stove.

I'm sure those who enjoy the rugged outdoors and are proficient at building fires must be laughing that it took some transplanted southern Arizonans so long to learn these simple lessons in Alaska. Yet many pastors and church leaders have not figured out some of the most basic principles for fanning the flames of the Holy Spirit in their churches. The church dwells in a cold world. God has given us what we need to create the warmth that will thaw hearts. God desires to set our churches afire with love. Are we willing to learn about the power of spiritual momentum?

Spiritual Momentum

What makes momentum spiritual as opposed to purely emotional? Athletic teams experience the incredible power of emotional momentum so that they play at a new level. Is this all we are talking about here? Shall the church tap into the principle of momentum simply because it works in other organizations?

The word *momentum* does not appear anywhere in the Bible. We cannot simply look up a particular Greek word in the New Testament or find the appropriate Hebrew word in the Old Testament. Instead, we must study the life lessons of God's leaders to note the power of momentum. Reading the Bible with a mind that is tuned to the idea of momentum, one discovers it pervades the pages of scripture.

Momentum turns out to be biblical, spiritual, and powerful. Several biblical leaders discovered that God's Spirit uses momentum to nurture God's people toward maturity and blessing. The lineup of biblical leaders who modeled clear momentum principles includes Hezekiah, Nehemiah, Moses, David, and Paul. Some lesser-known Bible characters remind us of the dangers of failure when momentum principles are broken. For those who have eyes to see, spiritual leaders are momentum leaders.

Biblical Leaders and Momentum

This book is organized around several key biblical leaders who can mentor us in the guiding principles of momentum. We start with Hezekiah, because he best exemplifies how a leader in tune with God can take God's people from dead spirituality to vibrant health and enthusiasm for God. Next, we will spend time with Nehemiah to clarify how to handle criticism and negativity when change begins to happen in a congregation. From there we will pause for a moment with Isaiah in the presence of God to discern the importance of carrying the coals of momentum from one ministry area to another.

Moses will mentor us in the importance of coordinating communications to keep a congregation moving with positive momentum. The apostles follow Moses in this leadership seminar as they took his principles a step further than he did. Whereas Moses saw the importance of coordinating communications among leaders, the apostles realized that the momentum of cooperation requires an affirmation of God's giving us diverse personalities to create a teamwork effort. The apostle Paul took this from mere cooperation into the strong momentum force of collaboration by calling the congregation a "body." But this wasn't a new insight with Paul. King David had discovered the power of servant-leadership as it applies to momentum. He also saw the failure of reverting to mere techniques such as using positive spin to generate momentum.

Finally, in the gospels, we see Jesus teaching momentum principles in his kingdom parables about growth. The kingdom of God is like growing plants that have a momentum all their own.

This book will help you explore the following momentum leadership principles drawn directly from the lives of biblical leaders:

1. You already have the resources you need for revival fires to be ignited in your congregation. You just need to identify them.

2. Generating momentum requires change. If your congregation is not experiencing growth and excitement in serving God, change something.

3. Positive congregational momentum expands in proportion to the congregants' expanded and deepened stewardship commitments.

4. Any change toward positive momentum will create an opposite pull to halt progress in a new direction. A momentum leader must know how to confront negativity and manage criticism.

5. Congregational momentum requires that the leader work to align the inherent reward system to the new culture desired.

6. Celebrating the new direction is a proactive way to minimize the power of grumblers and complainers.

7. Positive momentum in a congregation requires high-trust, face-to-face communications.

8. Congregational leaders help keep the momentum going when the pastor keeps them informed so they can stay ahead of the congregation.

9. Affirmation of diverse gifts and personalities helps a congregation move with momentum toward health and growth.

10. When congregational leaders collaborate, it energizes positive momentum.

11. Servant-leadership builds momentum by generating positive relationships and healthy teamwork.

12. Overly optimistic, positive messages endanger momentum because they tend to raise unrealistic expectations.

13. Because God's kingdom is expected to grow, pastors and congregational leaders need to stop making excuses for lack of momentum.

14. Momentum leaders need accountability partners as well as a healthy personal devotional life to keep the congregation moving in a positive direction.

CHAPTER 1

Hezekiah Gathers Kindling

Let me clarify how our second son was born in our kitchen. We had lived in an Alaskan village for only six weeks when Kathy went into labor. Because her labor started too late to catch the last evening flight off the island and get her to a hospital, we had to make do with no doctor or trained delivery staff. On top of that, I had not yet learned how to heat our little village house, so it remained in the high forties and low fifties that night. Desperate to keep the baby warm, we opened the door of the electric oven and heated the kitchen to deliver the baby.

Some additional background information might be helpful. Moving from southern Arizona to a mission church among the Tlinget people of Alaska was a wonderful, terrifying experience. We Arizonans, born and bred, packed up everything we owned and moved just before Thanksgiving to arrive at the village by the first week of December. We arrived to learn that the hot water heater in the parsonage had broken. The church had replaced it with a new, efficient, insulated hot water heater just in time for their new pastor. There was just one problem. The old water heater not only heated water but also was the major source of heat for the entire house. Unlike previous pastors, we had to rely entirely on the old broken oil stove in the dining room (with only one setting–cold) and an inefficient Franklin woodstove in the living room. Thus, I was introduced to the discipline of making a wood fire each morning to heat our house.

The first step of making a fire, as any Boy Scout knows, is to gather the kindling. Usually, gathering kindling means collecting some dead branches and breaking them into small pieces. I suppose that works when you are out in the woods surrounded by small dead branches. In our case, we had no dead branches nearby.

Our source of kindling was a recent donation of logs piled up in our back yard. Someone had cut a live tree and donated the wood to the local pastor. A nice gesture, but the donated wood was still green. (Not that I knew the difference between green wood and seasoned wood.) On top of that, the logs in the back yard were wet from lying out in the rain all fall. I did not think I had the resources I needed to build a fire. Most of December and January I seldom got the house temperature above sixty. I felt helpless, unprepared, and just plain stuck.

Staying Stuck

One of the most common reasons churches remain stuck in old patterns of negative inertia is that the leaders don't think they have the resources to do anything different. For most pastors and church leaders, the term *resource* equals "money." Just watch how your church leaders respond when someone in the congregation suggests your congregation develop a new ministry. What is the knee-jerk reaction in congregations that are stuck on a negative plateau? "That's nice, but we don't have the resources (money)." Here is the truth: We already have the resources required for momentum, but we don't know it. Instead, we struggle with spiritual depression.

Have you ever struggled with mild depression? I find it can settle in right after a significant accomplishment. For instance, one of the worst times I recall struggling with low-grade depression came right after I completed my doctorate. My focus had been so intensely on accomplishing the degree that I experienced a temporary letdown when it was done. What do I do now? I found myself sitting in front of the television and flipping channels late at night. I was going through the motions at the office, but without much excitement. I told myself I should be feeling on top of the world, but I could barely get out of bed in the mornings. How do we break this kind of mood?

The best way I know to break out of this kind of depression is to find a practical task that has closure in a relatively short time frame. It might be as small as rearranging furniture in the office. Cleaning off the desk and straightening the shelves can help get the juices flowing again. At home it might be trimming the hedges and mowing the lawn. The important thing is to do something, however small, that has a beginning and ending point. Why? Small accomplishments remind us of the abilities we already possess—our resources.

Too many church leaders are stuck in a form of low-grade depression—inertia. They are going through the motions, but their last significant accomplishment was so long ago that it might as well be ancient history. They are fulfilling the classic twelve-step definition of insanity: doing the same thing over and over while expecting different results.

At first it doesn't sound like that big of a deal. Everybody gets stuck sometimes. But when we stay stuck for months or even years, it signifies a serious problem. In fact, the ancient church considered this one of the seven deadly sins, known as *acedia*. The modern word for it is *sloth*. It essentially comes down to the thought "I don't care enough to do anything about it."

Inertia has a momentum all its own. It is easier to keep doing what we are already doing than to try something different. It takes effort to break the momentum of inertia.

Breaking the Momentum of Inertia

I am thinking of those Florida voters in the 2000 presidential election who accidentally cast their ballots for the wrong candidate. They experienced the natural results of the momentum of inertia. One woman commented after the election that her elementary-school–age son could read and follow the directions. Of course, he got it right. It was his first time to study a ballot. Those who had voted incorrectly were not first-time voters. They were people who had cast votes for years. They knew the routine. They did exactly the same thing they had done for years. The problem was that someone had redesigned the ballot.

The momentum of inertia saves us from wasting our energy having to consider every little thing we do. When was the last time we read the directions on a tube of toothpaste? How often do we read the directions on the shampoo bottle? Only people who are using these products for the first time read the directions. Once we have used a hygiene product a few times, we stop reading the directions. Momentum takes over. Inertia means we can go through the motions without thinking.

The problem in too many churches is that the momentum of inertia reflects a helpless attitude of negativity and now controls the church. As long as we continue doing the same things we did last month, we will keep getting the same results. Each congregation, like any organization, is perfectly aligned to get the results it is getting.

Here is where it gets tricky. Many churches are functioning in patterns that worked a generation ago but no longer work today. The orange shag carpet that was hip in the 1970s is out of step with the twenty-first century. Churches that functioned with minimal nursery facilities through the 1980s are now losing the opportunity to minister to young families without realizing it. Congregations whose primary strength was their denominational loyalty in the 1960s are out of step with the visitor who doesn't care what name is over the front door. When we get caught in patterns that worked a generation ago but are not producing the results we want now, we are stuck.

The sad truth is that most congregations who think they want new members do not really want to make the changes needed to attract new members. What they really want is for a new generation to come maintain the church the same way it's been done for fifty years. They want new resources invested in the same old ways. News flash! The younger generations are not interested in keeping our churches in the same old patterns. If we want them to come to our church, we'll have to be open to their bringing changes. I'm not talking about letting them change the basic gospel. The same gospel can be communicated in fresh interesting ways relevant to new people.

Changing the Momentum

If we want different results from what we are getting now, then we have do something to change the momentum. The answer is so simple we can easily miss it. Instead of hoping for more resources that can be spent in old ways, we can break the inertia by investing the same resources differently. Watch how Hezekiah did it.

King Hezekiah mastered the art of spiritual momentum. His story is told in 2 Chronicles 29–32. The spiritual temperature of his generation was not too different from ours. The flames of enthusiasm for God had nearly disappeared among the people of God. Their spiritually cold times could be seen by the fact that the temple in Jerusalem sat in disrepair. Rooms once used to hold worship supplies were filled with garbage, dust, and spider webs. Those few attending worship simply went through the empty, dutiful motions.

Hezekiah had a vision that it could and should be different. What Hezekiah did was no different from what we can do today. Once we understand the power of spiritual momentum, we can release our congregations from their negative habits. Instead of defending ourselves with "we are the faithful remnant" theology, we can stir our people to deeper joy and watch our churches grow healthy. Let's consider how Hezekiah initiated the spiritual renewal of his day.

Momentum, like fire, first requires kindling. Another way of saying this is that we need resources to bring about renewal. But the most valuable resources are not financial but human.

King Hezekiah realized he already had the kindling he needed for spiritual momentum. He had a more precious resource than money. He had the commitment of time, energy, and imagination from his spiritual leaders. Granted, he inherited a group of depressed priests and Levites. They were weary of doing the same old thing with little response. So Hezekiah decided to invest their energy and time differently. His assignment was intensely practical. "Carry out the filth from the holy place" (2 Chr. 29:5). He told them to clean the temple from top to bottom. They were to haul out the garbage, remove spider webs, and scrub the temple clean. In the process he broke their spiritual depression.

Hezekiah chopped the kindling for a spiritual revival by showing his people that they were not helpless victims. God's people could do something different from what they had put up with in the past. To break their frozen inertia, they started with a practical task: housecleaning. The entire task took them more than two weeks of concerted effort.

Relationships as Momentum Resources

How do we, like Hezekiah, discover the resources that could be redirected to build spiritual momentum? Start by thinking of the relationships we already have in the congregation.

I discovered the importance of relationships as a resource in that Alaskan village. It turned out I had way more resources for heating our home than simply the pile of green wood logs in our backyard. Although I was ignorant about making a wood fire, God provided me with knowledge shared by the elders who had made wood fires most of their lives. They wanted to help their new young pastor be successful. I don't know why it took me six weeks to ask for help. I guess I was making the same mistake most pastors make, thinking it was all up to me to figure it out. Once the elders knew I needed help, they not only shared their wood but also began teaching me about making a wood fire.

The kindling for your congregational momentum is not simply the traditions you inherited. Instead of focusing on your church's historic giving level, current budget, or bank account, why not see what other resources God has already given you? In other words, kindling consists of the vast resources of knowledge, wisdom, and experiences of your people.

Many large congregations like ours ran into serious financial problems in the economy that followed the tragedy of September 11, 2001. I know I was not the only head of staff pastor pleading in my prayers, "Lord, release more resources." Our finances were extremely tight. We had just completed a major capital expansion. We carried higher maintenance bills than previously. Fortunately, we did not have to let go of any staff as so many other larger churches did. We decided not to replace one of our retiring pastors and an assistant who resigned for family reasons. Thus, we limped along.

In the midst of those difficult times I prayed daily for God to release the resources we needed to do the ministry we were called to do. I'll admit that what I meant by that prayer was that I wanted more financial income. It didn't happen that way. Instead, God brought to us a new collection of incredibly gifted people. As one staff member was leaving her post, God prepared the heart of a senior vice-president of a very successful company to come to us. Hearing God's call, he left his six-figure income and came to work with us for about one-third of his former salary. A couple of recently retired college professors with Ph.D.s volunteered to lead our adult education programs. I eventually realized that God was answering my prayers. God did not give us more money but something much more precious—gifted people.

Time as a Momentum Resource

Resources are more about relationships than money. Once we realize this, it frees us for further "out-of-the-box" thinking. For instance, time is one of our most precious resources. We all have the same twenty-four hours in a day. But we can invest this resource in many different ways. Hezekiah told the priests to use their time differently. Instead of doing the same old things, they were assigned the task of cleaning the temple.

When it comes to pastors and congregational leaders, our people watch how we spend our time more than we realize. I discovered some years ago just how powerfully a leader's use of time models values and influences people. A few weeks after I arrived as the new head of staff at my current church, I volunteered in our church kitchen to wash dishes. We had finished our weekly Wednesday evening dinner for about two hundred people. After peeking in at a couple of the classes that evening, I returned to the kitchen and asked if I could help with the cleanup. I honestly did not think it was that big a deal. As far as I was concerned, it was a positive use of my time to get to know some of our volunteers. I could have spent that hour working in my office wading through some administrative paperwork. I chose to invest it with some of our kitchen crew and hospitality volunteers.

Little did I know how much one hour in the kitchen would influence the culture and expectations of the congregation. According to the conversations the next few weeks around our church, one would think I was an amazing leader. People kept talking about their new head of staff pastor doing dishes after a church supper. As the idea of servant-leadership took hold in our church, we stopped having to plead for volunteers to help in the Sunday school, to tutor children after school, or to help hammer nails for Habitat for Humanity. Over the next few years our church went from a culture of "department store shoppers" that expected the church to serve them to a culture of servant-leaders looking for opportunities to do ministry.

The kindling for momentum often involves reassessing and reinvesting our time according to new priorities. For instance, over the last couple of years we have redirected our staff meeting time. I inherited the tradition of weekly staff meetings used primarily for calendar coordination and announcements. If we wanted to shift our culture toward an emphasis on personal transformation, we not only needed to talk about it at staff meetings, but we needed to model it in our use of staff time. We realized that if we genuinely wanted our congregation to emphasize ongoing personal transformation and healthy relationships, then our staff had to live it first.

We intentionally designed a new monthly rhythm for our weekly staff meetings. While we continued using the first week of each month as our major coordination meeting, we extended it and made it more inclusive than in the past. We not only invite all the staff, instead of only the program staff, but we take the first hour to eat a leisurely staff breakfast so we can share around the tables. The second hour of that meeting is used less to coordinate calendar events and more to celebrate our successes as we move toward our vision. We laugh a lot and tell a lot of stories about people's lives being transformed through our various ministries.

The second and fourth weeks of the month involve a brief devotional time with the whole staff followed by small groups. Because our focus is on personal transformation, one of our pastors named these groups, "Transformation Accountability Groups," or TAG. Each small group of six to eight staff members intentionally includes people from different ministry areas. In these groups we share with one another how the Lord is working in our personal lives and pray for one another. The point of these groups is not simply to discuss our professional work, but also to intertwine family concerns in these high-trust, confidential groups. Our musicians pray with our administrative assistants. Our finance office people share with our youth workers. We intentionally work at building trust. Finally, we use the third weekly meeting to clarify any major concern or issue that needs to be addressed.

Our staff members invest similar amounts of time in staff meetings as were used in the past. But the emphasis has shifted dramatically by how much of this time we invest in building collaborative relationships. We work at building trust more than coordinating calendars. Same time, new priorities.

Creative Thinking as a Resource

If resources are about relationships and time more than dollars, then that frees us for further out-of-the-box thinking. Here is an easy test: Picture a glass partially filled with water. You know the traditional question: Is the glass half empty or half full? If the pessimist sees it as half empty, does that mean the optimist sees it as half full? Not necessarily. A truly creative optimist sees not only the water but also the incredible potential of the glass. Once the creative optimist stops focusing on the water level and instead considers what could be done with an empty glass, all kinds of wonderful options appear. Tip the glass upside down and use it as a support for a nice centerpiece. What if the glass were used as part of an art display? Instead of water, let's fill it with bows, or buttons, or candy. How about using it as a prop for a drama?

Entrepreneurial leaders usually enjoy momentum because they open their minds to all kinds of creative uses of the same resources that others keep using in the same old ways. This is true for how we see people in our congregation. For instance, our director of ministry opportunities saw Walter differently than the rest of our congregation saw him.

Walter started attending our church a couple of years ago. Unemployable due to mental disabilities, he enjoyed not only attending services with his family but also hanging around our campus. Many in the church were solicitous and kind to him. But expectations for him were low. Everyone saw him as a nice guy. But we didn't really believe that he had a ministry.

Angela, our director of ministry opportunities, interviewed Walter to see if she could help him find his ministry. Learning of his interest in helping around our campus, she set up a meeting between our facilities manager and this unemployable man. Now Walter volunteers one or two days every week to assist our custodians. He smiles at me every time I see him. He is fun to have around our campus. Last week, as I watched him sway to the music in the worship service, I was struck again with what a blessing he is. When he came to our church, God gave us a resource–not money. Walter gives us something much more valuable–himself.

Are You Fishing for Momentum Resources?

Many church leaders resonate with Peter and his fishing companions when they fished all night with no results. They did all the same things that had worked in the past. They worked the nets throughout the night. They went to the normal places where they had caught fish before. But this time they came up empty. Frustrated, they returned to shore and began washing their nets. Jesus arrived in the same area and began teaching a crowd of people on the shore. As the crowd grew, Jesus saw Peter's empty boat as a resource. When Jesus finished speaking, he invited Peter to take his freshly cleaned net and push out into the deep water. Jesus promised Peter would catch fish this time (Lk. 5).

Peter's first response was barely polite. He reminded Jesus that they had already spent the entire night without catching any fish. Peter was tired and probably wanted to catch some sleep during the day so he could repeat his attempts the next night. He wanted to stay in a routine he knew and trusted. So maybe it wasn't as effective as it had been in the past. Still, why try anything new? Jesus' invitation stood. Was Peter willing to take the same resources–his nets and boat– and try something new? What if he tried fishing in the daytime instead of in the traditional nighttime? Peter gave it a shot. He tossed the nets in and caught so many fish it took two boats to haul them to shore.

You already have the resources you need to break out of your current congregational inertia. Just as Peter already had his boat and nets as well as his strength and fishing ability, you have your people's time and energy–their intelligence and imagination. All you need to do is redirect these wonderful resources.

CHAPTER 2

Hezekiah Strikes a Spark

A few years ago, one of our members invited my wife and me to lunch. The hostess and host wanted to introduce us to another pastor and his wife. They explained in the invitation that they appreciated both of our ministries and wanted us to meet one another. Kathy and I agreed. Our hostess seated us carefully around the table and then said to me: "I want to start our lunch today by asking Bruce to lead us in communion." I looked down and realized I was the only one who had a dinner roll and a glass of grape juice in front of me.

Now, according to my denomination, turning that lunch into a communion service involved my breaking a whole bunch of rules. Our denomination does not practice communion without a reading of scripture and explanation of the Word. Further, only ordained pastors approved by our denomination are allowed to break the bread at the Lord's table. The other pastor, with ordination in a different tradition, would not be allowed to lead a communion service at our church. And when communion is served off campus, such as at a retreat or conference, we require the approval of our elders. We have these rules and more. Our hostess was asking me to break most of them.

She had no idea she was asking me to break a bunch of denominational rules. She was just trying to make our time together special. The other pastor looked knowingly at me, smiled broadly, and waited to see what I would do. My wife glanced at me with a look that meant, "So, how are you going to get out of this?" I silently prayed: "Holy Spirit, how do I make Jesus smile in this situation?" Then I took the dinner roll, broke it, and said, "Jesus told us to do this in remembrance of him." And I think Jesus smiled.

The Momentum of Risk

Hezekiah knew that God cares more about grace than rules, more about people than policies. He knew what we as church leaders often ignore—perfectionism can kill momentum. We need to ask ourselves, Is it more important that we perfectly abide by the rules of our denomination or that people encounter our living Lord? Is it more important that we maintain our traditions or that people experience grace? Sometimes we need to make exceptions to the rules to minister more effectively to people as well as to generate momentum.

Momentum, like fire, involves risk. You get no warmth from simply stacking kindling in the corner; you have to set a spark to the kindling. But this is a risky action. The same is true of momentum. If you want it, you must be willing to take the risk.

King Hezekiah recognized this when he announced the grand reopening of the temple in Jerusalem. He included a Passover celebration in his plans because he felt it would stir the people's imagination. However, plans for the holiday grew so elaborate that he was forced to delay the Passover until a month later than the traditional date—a truly risky decision.

Can you imagine moving the church's traditional Christmas Eve services to January 24? What pastor would want to stand before the congregation and announce, "Our choir director has planned some really exciting Christmas music, but the choir needs an extra month to rehearse"? Or what would happen if the chair of your church building committee announced, "Renovations on the sanctuary won't be completed by Easter, so we're recommending that we postpone Easter services until May"? How would your church board react to this recommendation?

Hezekiah announced that the Passover celebration would be a month late! The response was exactly what you'd expect. When the messengers went from town to town with the news of the month delay for Passover, most of the people "laughed them to scorn, and mocked them" (2 Chr. 30:10). But Hezekiah used the delay to spark spiritual momentum. Everybody was talking about the news. It had been so long since they'd had a traditional Passover celebration that people were curious. They even looked more closely at what Passover required of them. Many of the leaders had not properly prepared themselves for the Passover according to Moses' laws. The question arose, Should the Passover be canceled due to the lack of purity preparations?

Their curiosity and questioning only fueled King Hezekiah's determination. He went ahead with the Passover, praying that God would graciously accept all those who had not properly purified themselves. He wanted them included in the holiday celebrations. "But Hezekiah prayed for them, saying, 'The good LORD pardon all who set their hearts to seek God...'" (2 Chr. 30:18). For Hezekiah, the people and their relationship to God were more important than the rules. Are we willing to go against tradition or even to do something wrong when it will help people experience the Lord's touch in their lives? Are we willing to take that kind of risk?

Look what happened when King Hezekiah changed the traditional time for observing Passover and allowed ritually unpurified people to eat the Passover meal. (2 Chr. 30:20). Passover became such an exciting event that the people asked that it continue for a second week. Instead of the normal seven days of Passover, they turned it into a fourteen-day event. "Then the whole assembly agreed together to keep the festival for another seven days; so they kept it for another seven days with gladness" (2 Chr. 30:23).

Remember, this revival began when the worship leaders scrubbed the temple clean. This provided the kindling for the fire. But the Passover celebration furnished the necessary spark to get the fire started. It was a risky thing to do, but it was just what was needed to jolt people out of their spiritual lethargy.

Risks and Short-term Wins

Hezekiah was creating what John Kotter calls "short-term wins." In his book *Leading Change,* Kotter proposes that short-term wins are a necessary step in any major organizational transformation. He defines short-term wins as visible, unambiguous, and clearly related to the change being implemented. He maintains that, in the corporate setting, people are hesitant to sacrifice for a larger dream unless they see some immediate small accomplishments in their current reality.

Short-term wins reinforce the credibility of the leader as well as the direction of the leader's big dreams.[1]

Church leaders would do well to learn this lesson from the corporate world. Just as corporate leaders need a big vision that is sustained by short-term wins, so congregational leaders who believe in the big vision of bringing the gospel to the whole world also need local short-term wins. For example, twice a year I meet with three fellow pastors of large successful churches in our denomination. The main point of our meetings is to encourage one another to dream bigger dreams. We light up one another's imaginations. We push one another to excellence. We take risks and hold one another accountable to try something new. We offer one another the grace to experiment and fail in the name of growth.

At a recent meeting we spent the first day sharing the new experiments we were each trying and what was working or not working. One pastor reported on how his preaching style had changed to match a new service they had added to their Sunday morning schedule. Another told how he was canceling Sunday worship once a quarter to take his congregation on field trips to worship in different settings. These colleagues are out-of-the-box thinkers! The second day we shared insights from books we had each read about ways to promote healthy church growth. We also shared family and personal concerns and joys as part of our prayer time together. Near the end of our time, one of the pastors asked his traditional question, "What one or two specific things are each of you going to do as a result of this time together?" And so, in the midst of our big dreams, we each set specific goals to do something new and achieve some small wins. After we go our separate ways, we frequently check in to hold one another accountable.

Small wins are vital in sparking spiritual momentum. Yes, leadership materials constantly remind us that leaders are to dream big and take bold risks to accomplish their bold vision. But it takes small wins to break the inertia of what is already comfortable and familiar. Leaders like Hezekiah, who understood the power of spiritual momentum, combine small changes with their bold, challenging vision. If you're not this kind of leader, don't despair. It took me years to learn how to use momentum, but I assure you that the skills of momentum can be learned.

---

[1]John Kotter, *Leading Change* (Boston: Harvard Business School Press, 1996), 121–22.

Risk Taking as a Learned Skill

For twenty of my twenty-five years of ministry I have had the joy of serving healthy, growing ministries. But my first pastoral experience was radically different. I struggled in a church that was in a downward spiral, and I hadn't a clue about what to do. The church had one hundred members when I started and about ninety members when I left three years later. I faithfully preached and taught the scriptures. I ran meetings and desperately tried to hold onto what we already had. I realize now that I lacked vision. I am not naturally a visionary, so I was stuck and the church was stuck in doing the same things we'd always done. The end result was decline—decline in average attendance and decline in giving. And the hopes with which I'd arrived three years earlier plummeted as well. It wasn't fun.

A terrible tragedy represented my lack of skills at understanding ministry in general and momentum in specific. It happened during my second year of ministry in that little Alaskan village. I recall the look in a mother's eyes as she asked me, "Pastor, would you baptize our children before their funeral?" This question presented one of the toughest dilemmas I faced at that Alaskan village church. Fresh out of seminary, I was steeped in the complexities of reformed theology on infant baptism. How should I explain to the grieving family that baptism was not necessary for their children to go to heaven?

The house had caught fire in the middle of the night. The uncle, who was supposed to keep an eye on the children, had fallen asleep. When the fire went out in the woodstove, the two young children had tried to get it started again without waking him. At least that's what the police thought had happened. The firefighters rushed into the inferno in time to rescue the uncle, but the two children were already dead.

By the time I became part of the story, the children's bodies were end-to-end in an adult casket; and I was faced with a decision. Of course, I was touched by the family's grief and wanted to alleviate their hurt. But I still had to refuse their request because it was against all our denominational policies. I did my best to assure them that their children were already with God in heaven. But I still have a haunting feeling that they saw my actions as a rejection without appreciating my theology.

By the third year in that village church I seriously considered leaving the ministry. I applied for positions in other fields, but no door opened. Anxious to be out of this unhappy situation, I accepted a position as an interim chaplain at a very small denominational college as a first step toward an eventual teaching career. Only after I made a couple of key decisions in this campus ministry did I happen upon the power of spiritual momentum. These decisions significantly revitalized this ministry. Momentum grew from good decisions and small wins. And my ministry has never been the same

The turning point for me came when I had nothing to lose by agreeing to serve one year as an interim chaplain at this small college campus with less than two hundred students. The chapel services my first year averaged around ten students and two faculty members. Five years later our chapel attendance was more than fifty students and often included at least ten faculty members. This turnaround was, in large part, sparked by an experiment with the meeting time of our mid-week Bible study. Instead of continuing the traditional 7 p.m. Bible study that was comfortable for the faculty, staff, and me, we let the students suggest a time they would prefer to attend. Certainly, this was a risky thing to do. The results weren't entirely to my liking: They asked me to move the weekly Bible study to 10:10 p.m. on Tuesday evenings. Inwardly, I groaned: "10:10–that's my bedtime!" But we tried it anyway.

The numbers for the 10:10 p.m. Bible study grew quickly. We discovered that most of the college students were more awake between 10 p.m. and midnight than they were the rest of the day. Allowing the students to set their own times for activities empowered them to own the ministries and share their faith with others. Once students felt empowered to grow their own ministries on that campus, momentum developed.

I moved from that college to a stable, solid church with 150 worshipers with an average age in the upper sixties. Twelve years later we had built and paid for a new sanctuary, office, and Christian education complex. Our attendance had tripled to 450. The budget had simultaneously more than tripled, and mission giving had quadrupled. This congregation had achieved momentum.

As I look back on the exciting time with this congregation, I realize that this momentum was sparked largely when we took the risk of changing our Sunday morning schedule to be more attractive to young families. We added a new worship service with an overlapping Sunday school program at 9:30 a.m., even though the actual worship attendance numbers did not justify such an action. Many faithful, long-time members wondered why we didn't simply ask people to move from the full 11:00 a.m. service to the 8:30 a.m.

service to balance attendance at both services. Instead, we created a new third service. And the risk paid off!

Seizing Opportunities for Risk Taking

Sometimes unintended changes occur that force us to take new risks. It's important to be alert to the opportunities and to seize them. Again, I speak from experience. When our oldest son was a junior in high school, he didn't wake up one morning. He had slipped into an encephalitis coma. Over the next couple of days we prayed that God would spare his life. He finally awoke but had serious brain damage resulting from the trauma to his brain. Moreover, the prognosis for the future was uncertain. For several months, our congregation prayed for his healing and, in the process, pulled together into a wonderful healing community. Thankfully, our son eventually recovered.

We discovered during this trying time what Joseph had learned in Egypt: What may start out appearing as evil, God can turn into good (Gen. 50:20). This medical crisis turned into a spark of momentum that moved our church in a whole new direction. For instance, our son's illness radically affected my prayer life. I developed a new boldness in asking the Lord for miracles. Our mainline church started a new healing ministry and began holding regular healing services—not only for physical recovery, but also for broken relationships and wounded emotions. It was a risk, because many mainline members view healing services as something "they" (mostly Pentecostals) do, not something "we" do. The risk paid off, however, in a meaningful new ministry. The unintended (and unwanted) spark was a medical crisis, but the resulting flame was our new healing ministry.

Six years ago, I moved on to my current ministry. Once again I inherited a solid, stable church that had averaged more than one thousand worshippers for twenty years. After a hurtful split in the church, my predecessor, a very caring pastor, nurtured the congregation back to health. It had consistent worship attendance and had active youth, music, education, fellowship, and missions programs. This church was active, solid, but not growing.

However, things changed. We recently celebrated a successful six-million-dollar expansion campaign to increase our sanctuary and youth space. Average attendance has grown from eleven hundred to eighteen hundred. We have purchased additional land to develop a second campus. All this has resulted from taking some huge risks.

The biggest risk of my first two years here came when we decided to add a new contemporary service on Sunday morning at a time that overlapped a traditional service. To preach at all five weekend services, I had to juggle my schedule. I preached at the new service in the fellowship hall while other staff members started the sanctuary worship service. I was placed early in the contemporary worship in the fellowship hall so that as soon as I finished preaching there, I could quickly don a robe and move to the sanctuary to preach at the traditional service. During the first year attendance grew from zero to three hundred in that new worship service. Now, attendance at that service is more than five hundred. Our previous ministry style has remained solid. The growth has been mostly as a result of taking the risk of starting a new service.

Will You Risk Changing the Thermostat for Momentum?

On the one hand, I don't believe that counting numbers validates ministries. The staff in this church has heard me say many times that I care less about how many people come to our events and more about what God is doing to transform their lives. I would rather have five people who are genuinely encountering Jesus Christ than a crowd of people who are only playing games with God.

On the other hand, numbers can be used as a thermometer for determining the temperature of a congregation. Struggling churches often fool themselves into thinking they are doing well when they are simply going through the motions. They pride themselves on their friendliness, when they are only friendly to their own inner circle. Their numbers show they are stuck in maintenance ministries and lack vitality. Such numbers are very revealing. They can help us pay attention to the thermostat—the spiritual momentum that effectively raises the warmth in a church.

If I had to do it over again, I would baptize those two village children in the casket—even though it's contrary to our theology and tradition. I've come to the point in my ministry where I worry less about the rules and look more into people's eyes. I am more willing to take risks to bring people into a vibrant relationship with Jesus. As much as Jesus risked for us, how much are we willing to risk for him?

CHAPTER 3

Hezekiah Adds Fuel to the Fire

I love God's sense of humor. In the interviews for my current church, someone on the selection committee asked why I would leave my former ministry, given its exciting, vibrant congregation. I explained that the congregation had grown over ten years to the size we dreamed it could be. We had met all our goals for that ministry, and now I was ready for some new challenges.

In our former congregation the next step of growth would have required the purchase of additional property to begin another church in the community. I was not fired up about buying property or building a new church. I didn't view that as either something that was one of my strengths or as something I was called to do. It seemed perfectly reasonable, therefore, that it was time to move on. So I smiled as I responded comfortably to the questions.

Still, I felt some inner unease. I recall commenting to my wife that evening, "Wouldn't it be weird if I came here and then had to face the same decisions about growing and expansion that we're leaving behind?" In my heart, I saw that there was no escaping from God's big vision.

The Sacrifice Momentum Requires

When our current church began to grow significantly, I reminded the Lord that I had already led two capital expansions in our previous church. Couldn't this church just grow in slow, healthy ways that wouldn't require another building expansion and major campaign? The Lord showed me the same thing that he'd revealed to Hezekiah. If we put in place the dynamics of spiritual momentum, God's renewal spreads like wildfire. The leaders get excited about what God is doing among and through the congregation. God's people are drawn to deeper commitments. Guess what happens next? In most settings, God pushes the congregation to consider what they would be willing to give up to participate more fully in God's exciting kingdom.

What is your congregation ready to sacrifice for spiritual renewal? A friend who consults with churches on capital campaigns suggests that if a congregation has gone longer than five years without a major financial campaign that stretches its members beyond the demands of their annual budget, it is probably growing stagnant. (Of course, he makes his living by running financial campaigns.) I'm not ready to go this far. However, I do believe that to promote spiritual momentum, a congregation needs a call to a major commitment requiring them to clarify their priorities in the name of a larger goal at least every ten years.

King Hezekiah knew the initial enthusiasm would die if he did not intentionally add fuel to the fire. Cleaning the temple and celebrating the double Passover had invigorated God's people for a short while, but Hezekiah knew something more was needed for a continued spiritual awakening. So he took the next step by calling the people to give even more to the Lord, which would require them to face those things that tended to control them—their idols. Their new devotion to the Lord needed to be lived out not only on holidays but also in their daily lives. The evidence that their new devotion was genuine is seen in the fact that they began giving in a way they had not formerly done.

Let's be honest, calling the congregation to deepen their commitment by contributing more of their resources usually scares church leaders. It is one reason we are hesitant to promote genuine spiritual renewal. We'll pray for revival and renewal, of course. However, most pastors hesitate to ask the congregational leaders to actually confront the idolatry of their lives to release the resources they have been squandering in selfish ways. How many pastors do this in their own lives?

Israel's revival started in the lives of the leaders before it spread to the rest of the congregation. "King Hezekiah of Judah gave the assembly a thousand bulls and seven thousand sheep for offerings, and the officials gave the assembly a thousand bulls and ten thousand sheep" (2 Chr. 29:24).

Sacrificing Our Idols

It is significant that in Hezekiah's story the release of financial resources coincided with his confronting idolatry.

> Now when all this was finished, all Israel who were present went out to the cities of Judah and broke down the pillars, hewed down the sacred poles, and pulled down the high places and the altars throughout all Judah and Benjamin, and in Ephraim and Manasseh, until they had destroyed them all. (2 Chr. 31:1)

Not only did they confront the public idolatry in their communities, they faced the idolatry within their own hearts. The easiest way to uncover our own idols is to review how we spend our resources of time, energy, and money. Where our treasure is, there will our hearts be also.

The reason a financial campaign adds fuel to the fire of spiritual momentum is that it is a very practical way of getting people to examine their own spiritual lives. It is often a time in which God tests the willingness of congregational members to give up something that has begun to control their lives in order to free them to go deeper in their intimacy with God. Let me illustrate with a few stories from a capital campaign we held a few years ago.

Prayer and Openness to Sacrifice

The major focus of that campaign was prayer, not money. We emphasized the need for each congregant to be disciplined in daily prayer for several weeks prior to any financial commitments. We asked people to pray, asking the Lord what God's will was for them in regard to their giving something of themselves to the future of the church. Of course, the only way we could give more of ourselves to God was to eliminate something that currently was important in our lives. The congregation spent weeks in prayer, seeking God's priorities for their lives.

One congregant had a poster in his garage of a fancy new car with all the bells and whistles. For some time he had dreamed of getting that car as a symbol of his success in business. But the poster came down once he began praying about his part in the church's capital expansion. He admitted that expensive cars tended to become idols in his life. He offered his dreams for the car back to the Lord. He told God he would only buy the car when he could accept it clearly as God's gift rather than as a symbol of his achievements.

Sacrifices and Healed Homes

One woman prayerfully concluded that God wanted her to give financially to the capital expansion. The problem was that her husband had nothing to do with our church. How could she meet God's request that she give of her finances when her husband had no interest in participating with our congregation? As she opened her life prayerfully to God, the Lord reminded her of a secret savings account she had hidden from her husband years before. When she had married this man ten years earlier, she was fearful whether he would treat her son from a previous marriage well. So she had hidden money in a savings account "just in case." She came to the point where she was willing to give up that secret account as her act of trust in the Lord. But God wasn't finished with her. The Holy Spirit whispered to her that she also needed to confess her lack of trust to her husband and why she was giving up that secret account. God promised to take her marriage relationship to a new level of trust and intimacy.

Later she wrote to me about what God had done in her life as a result of her releasing the funds for the capital campaign. "Little by little God revealed to me how I had been sabotaging my relationship with both my husband and my son by holding on to this 'control' account...God showed me how I had assisted my husband's stubbornness because we were not working together to work things out with my son." She concluded by describing how God was continuing to work on her "control tendencies" not only in her marriage but also in other areas of her life. She recognized her tendency to volunteer in the church only where she could control the situation. Now she was learning to be a better team player in congregational ministries. She concluded with a comment that God had blessed her with a new kind of peace. Her transformation came as a result of being challenged to pray about what God would have her give up to participate in our church's growth and expansion.

One woman, after praying about her part in the church expansion, wanted to include her less active husband in her considerations about what they might give financially. Her suggestion upset him—he felt she was already too generous to the church. He had hopes of early retirement and felt she was subverting his plans for their future. The argument became so hurtful that they barely talked for two weeks. The next time they spoke, he apologized for his overreaction. She then took the conversation in a new direction. "I just would like to know one thing. Am I a partner in this marriage, or am I simply the one who manages *your* money?" Her risky candor and personal vulnerability took their relationship to a new level of candor. Today they celebrate not only their fulfillment of a financial commitment that grew their faith but also the way God used it to cement their marriage.

A mother in our church sat down with the family budget. She spread it out on the floor and prayed over it line by line. What was God asking her to give up to release some resources for the church? She started by praying over their house mortgage. She asked God if they were supposed to give up their home and move to something smaller or cheaper. No, that didn't seem to be what God was telling her to do. After a couple hours of intense prayer, she still had no clear sense of any area of sacrifice that would symbolize a shift in priorities to make God the center of their lives.

At lunchtime she repeated the prayer procedure. Her husband was jogging during his lunch break. This time she came to the line for their daughter's tuition at a private Christian elementary school. God whispered to her to release that account for the church's future ministry and instead enroll their daughter in public school. Meanwhile her husband was hearing the same thing while out jogging. Without talking to each other that afternoon, they came to the same decision. It was time to put their daughter into public school and use those funds for the church.

I watched them tell this story before a group. The mother began to weep as she said, "I felt like God was calling me to do what Abraham did, making me sacrifice our daughter. I kept asking God if this was really what we were to do. Then God asked me if I was trusting our daughter to the Lord or to private school." Previously they had thought that having their daughter in a private Christian school was the same thing as trusting her to the Lord. Now both mother and father realized that the private school was becoming an idol in their lives.

Like Gideon, that mother admitted she lacked the faith to simply step out and do it. So she asked God for clear signs that this was really of the Lord and not simply her own imagination. God soon reinforced the message through a combination of events. Her husband came home and told about hearing God tell him to release the same funds. Later that week, she was shopping at a Christian bookstore when she spotted a magazine with a lead article about how to trust your children to the Lord. The clincher, however, came when she attended a neighborhood tea party, only to discover that most of the women in the room not only worked at the local public school where her daughter would attend but were committed Christians. She realized that God would take good care of their daughter, but their confidence needed to be in the Lord, not in the expensive private school.

Sacrifices Pointing to God's Provision

In my own prayers for this campaign God confronted a similar idolatry in my own life. I sensed God calling us to a financial figure that seemed too large for us to meet. In fact, it was equal to the portion of college education expenses that we intended for one of our children. Although we had never planned on paying our children's entire college expenses, we had planned to help each one get through the first couple years of college. I argued with God about what this meant. I reasoned that our children would not be able to succeed in life if they didn't complete college. Then God gently whispered to me, "Bruce, would you rather they have a college education or know me?" This should be an easy one. However, I hesitated before answering. Something deep inside me wasn't sure our children could be successful simply by trusting the Lord.

When the wrestling match of prayer ended and I submitted to God's wonderful embrace, Kathy and I committed to a pledge beyond our means. The next year our daughter surprised us with her choice of colleges. She decided to return to the small college where I had taught in Alaska. She received scholarship funds equal to the amount we had pledged to our church's capital campaign. Today, we celebrate that God cares for our children's future even more than we do. (Only one has finished in the traditional four years. The others vary from a seven-year to a twenty-year plan with marriage and children in the midst of it.)

Stewardship as Provision

I know that preaching and teaching about stewardship commitment is uncomfortable. I'm not saying it is the spark or the kindling for the momentum fire in your congregation. But I am suggesting it is the log required to keep the fire burning once the kindling has caught the flame.

Stewardship is a key to spiritual renewal and momentum. Maybe our problem is that we go about stewardship in the wrong way. We tend to focus only on what people will give up in their commitment to the church and often fail to reveal the wonderful process of God's provision. Let's take some of the sting out of stewardship.

King Hezekiah understood that calling our people to tithe and commit beyond their level of comfort opens God's provisions for the future. When he called the people of Israel to give, they "gave in abundance the first fruits of grain, wine, oil, honey, and of all the produce of the field; and they brought in abundantly the tithe of everything" (2 Chr. 31:5). In fact, they took their tithing commitment so seriously that a few months later Hezekiah discovered mounds of grain offerings along with heaps of olives and other kinds of supplies. He was pleased to discover that these offerings were the tithes given to the Lord. In fact, he built additional storerooms onto the temple to hold all these extra supplies (2 Chr. 31:5–11).

As these flames of renewal spread like wildfire, the people fell in love with God, turned away from their former idols, and gave to the Lord with fresh generosity. In fact, they overwhelmed the leaders of the temple with the size of their offerings. They did not realize that this revival was God's providential preparation for the greatest spiritual test of their generation. The storehouses were barely completed when Hezekiah faced the biggest challenge of his leadership–the invasion of the Assyrian army.

"King Sennacherib of Assyria came and invaded Judah" (2 Chr. 32:1). This was the same army that had destroyed the Northern Kingdom of Israel. The Assyrians not only conquered Israel, but they also destroyed the outlying villages of Judah. Then the Assyrians surrounded the city of Jerusalem. King Sennacherib's strategy was simple. He intended to starve the residents of Jerusalem by keeping them closed inside their city without access to supplies. Such siege warfare was a common tactic in ancient times. Soon Hezekiah and his people would be forced to accept defeat. All the Assyrians had to do was wait outside the walls and keep Israel trapped inside (2 Chr. 32:9-23).

This tactic didn't work. Months later, the Assyrian army gave up their siege and retreated. Jerusalem was saved. It doesn't take a rocket scientist to realize what had happened. The people of Jerusalem had given faithfully of their produce for months leading up to the attack by Assyria. They had built and filled storerooms with tithes given to God. Then, while Sennacherib sat outside the walls of Jerusalem, guess how God provided for them? You got it. The Lord returned to them in their time of crisis what they had given to the Lord in their times of prosperity…the tithes.

The Tithe as God's Social Security System

Here is a biblical principle of giving. The tithe is God's social security system. The way it works is that we give the tithe as our act of faithfulness. Then God multiplies it and returns it to us in our time of need. Although God may occasionally give us the same money we gave away, more often God gives us a different resource–relationships. The tithe is God's way of inviting us to live our lives in healthy, interdependent relationships. Either we can try to take care of ourselves by building personal savings to cover every possible contingency in our future, or we can give our tithe to the Lord and then trust God to multiply our resources by bringing us into healthy relationships in which others abound in the resources we lack.

A divorced mother came into my office recently. She was desperate. She had lost her job months ago and had spent her savings account taking care of herself and her children. Now she was dependent on her mother's help just to pay the bills. She posed her frustrations in the form of theological questions and complaints. "Where is God? I prayed and asked the Lord for help. I have the education and experience to work. I am a hard worker. But nothing has opened up in my field. Doesn't God promise to care for the widows and orphans? Why doesn't God answer my prayers?" She made it clear she didn't want a handout from the church; she wanted God to get her a job!

After nearly a half hour of listening to her, I posed a question. "What resources do you have to help you move forward?" She acted as though I hadn't heard her earlier description of her situation. "I've used all my savings. I don't have any more money." I nodded that I understood and then gently asked again. "Think with me about what resources you have. Your mom is helping, right?"

"Yes, but I don't think it's fair for her to keep helping me. I want to work."

I then repeated my question. "What resources do you already have that can help you discover new options?"

With her master's degree and years of experience in social work, she couldn't see her own situation. Finally, I answered my own question. "I think you have all kinds of relationship resources that you are not using. You're stuck because you're thinking of your options through the limited perspective of your educational credentials and work history. Why not look around and see what other resources God is providing?"

I saw it in her eyes the moment she got it. "Actually, I know a lot of people around this church. I've been embarrassed to tell them about my situation. I haven't asked for help. You're right! I thought I had to solve my problems all by myself." By the time she left, she had put together a plan for drawing on the relationships of the congregation.

Sacrificing Individualism for Community

Why is sacrificial giving an important component in building momentum? God wants us to give enough of our finances that we are desperate to build relationships. Tithers learn to think of their resources in a broader way than non-tithers. Non-tithers generally think about their future in very individualistic ways. "I can't afford to tithe because I need to save enough for possible medications and hospitalizations. What if I require home health care?" Tithers understand that no savings account is big enough to cover all such contingencies. Further, the medical profession knows that people who are highly connected in social support structures need less medical attention and recover more quickly. It's no surprise that God invites us to trade our individualistic view of financial security for the broader resources of loving relationships. As congregation members, we adopt one another as extended family.

I told you that my wife and I struggled with God's calling us to pledge an amount that would equal college savings for one of our four children. Yes, it was scary. I am sure it was harder for Kathy than for me. She watches our family expenses and worries more than I do about the practicalities of paying the bills. But we prayed and agreed to the commitment. Today, having completed our commitment before we gear up for the next capital expansion, I can testify that God has provided in wonderful ways.

One of our sons, in graduate school across the country, recently had an emotional meltdown. As a request for prayer went through our church, some good friends in the congregation called to offer a resource they wanted to give to us. "Bruce, we have a free frequent flier ticket on Southwest Airlines. Why don't you go spend some time with your son?" I thanked them for the kind offer and agreed to use their ticket. That time with our son was the best father-son time we have had in at least ten years. I was able to enjoy the moment of his spiritual return to Christ after five years of his having walked away from his relationship with Jesus. When I returned, I loved sharing with our friends how their prayers and gift of a travel ticket created a transformational moment in our son's life.

Stewardship as the Building of Relationships

Stewardship serves as the log for the fires of momentum. Stewardship is really about relationships, not money. Finances are just the means for people to enjoy building relationships. Just listen to Bob's story. Bob had seen a recent e-mail circulating through some of our church groups asking for gifts to keep one of our after-school clubs going until the end of the school year. The request was for $700. Bob felt led by the Holy Spirit to donate the entire amount. When he sent his e-mail saying he wanted to cover the mission need, he mentioned his wife who had died two years previously. "I think Susan would approve."

Someone who read his e-mail misunderstood his reference to Susan and assumed he intended the gift as a memorial gift in Susan's name. Bob hadn't meant it that way, but that is how it was taken. For a moment he was a little hurt that people might assume his intent was to give a memorial gift when he had genuinely felt a nudge from the Holy Spirit to make the contribution. In fact, when he sat down to write the check, he felt the Holy Spirit instruct him to round it off to an even $1,000. So he did. He sent the gift and received a nice thank you.

A short time later he received a letter from someone he didn't know who lived in another state. Bob opened the letter and discovered it was from an old friend of Susan's. The woman had written that she had never sent anything when Susan died and felt that God was telling her to send this memorial gift in Susan's name. She encouraged Bob to use it as Susan would have wanted. The check was for $1,000!

That's not the end of the story. I asked Bob's permission to use his story in a stewardship sermon later that spring. He agreed, and I told the congregation about Bob's experience of how God takes care of us when we step out in faith. A woman in our congregation caught me after church to tell me her response to Bob's story. "Bruce, I felt the Holy Spirit tell me to give $1,000 to that homework club project a few days before Bob, and I told the Lord I would do it as soon as I had some finances rearranged. I missed the opportunity to be obedient and forgot all about it until I heard your story today."

The next week she gave the church a check for $1,500. She explained that the additional $500 was her way of showing the Lord she wanted to be more faithful in responding to the Holy Spirit's nudge in the future. When I told Bob that his story had released more funds, he smiled and added, "This is not for your sermon, but my daughters challenged me after your sermon to give away the other

$1,000 instead of thinking of it as God's replacing the donation. I prayed about it and just learned that a friend is going into the mission field this summer. I gave him the other $1,000."

I love God's economy. God takes our financial tithes and multiplies them into relationship provisions for the future. God takes our individualistic tendencies to think we must solve our own problems and invites us into the joy of community of care. Hezekiah understood these momentum principles and used them to stir the flames of renewal.

Hezekiah knew that spiritual renewal and momentum never go unchallenged. With enemies on the horizon, he prayed for renewal and prepared his people for battle. If we take clear steps toward renewal, we had better also prepare for the momentum battles we will face as others try to stop the changes we are instituting. Once we see our people growing in their trust for the Lord, how do we protect what we have accomplished against those who want to kill our spiritual momentum?

Will You Ask Your People to Sacrifice for Momentum?

What is the idolatry that you and your congregation need to confront? When Jesus appeared in his resurrection body to Peter, he asked the question, "Simon son of John, do you love me more than these?" (Jn. 21:15). Jesus was challenging Peter to make an important decision. Would Peter be willing to give up everything that was so important to him to follow Jesus? When was the last time you asked your congregation to do this?

I recall a member of our congregation shaking hands with me one Sunday morning at the door. His response to my forthright call to greater commitment on the part of our people was surprising. "Pastor," he said as he leaned closer to be sure he had my undivided attention. "When my country called me to put my life on the line and even sacrifice it in World War II, I signed up. My country asked, and I stepped up to the commitment. To be honest, I would have done as much for my church. Until today, my church had never asked."

CHAPTER 4

Nehemiah Manages the Air Flow

During our first year in Alaska we learned that there is more to heating a home than simply sparking the kindling in the woodstove. The woodstove, an invention of Benjamin Franklin, is designed to radiate heat with high efficiency–a huge improvement over the inefficient open fireplace where most of the heat goes up the chimney with the smoke. The key to its efficiency involves controlling the draft of air going into the woodstove. If too much air blows on the fire, the flames either are blown out or the wood is consumed too quickly, while most of the heat escapes out the chimney. However, if too little air blows into the stove, then the fire smothers from lack of oxygen. Not enough air can also cause a creosote buildup in the chimney, leading to dangerous chimney fires. Thus, getting the air to flow properly is not only a necessity; it's also an art. When the woodstove is working efficiently, it can radiate amazing heat.

When she was well into her eighties, Kathy's grandmother visited us one snowy Christmas. We quickly realized that we had a problem when she couldn't get warm enough and insisted on spending nearly every waking hour a few feet from the woodstove in our living room. For Grandma's benefit, we kept a roaring fire burning continuously. She was happy, but the rest of the family was sweltering.

Because none of us, other than Grandma, could take the heat for more than fifteen minutes, we agreed to take turns sitting with her. We rotated faithfully to her side for our assigned shift. As sweat beaded on our foreheads, she sat contentedly near the woodstove wrapped in a blanket. She appreciated each time one of us opened the woodstove and added another log. "Thank you. It is so comfortable in here."

About mid-afternoon one of our children, who was just completing her turn with Grandma, laughingly invited the rest of us to notice the candles in the living room. The candles, nicely displayed in an Advent wreath, were listing seriously to one side and by evening had drooped all the way over into a posture of abject submission to the heat.

Just as we learned that the key to efficient use of our woodstove required setting the airflow properly, so the handling of criticism in the midst of church changes is an important momentum skill. I believe that criticism is to momentum what air is to a fire in the woodstove. Hurtful criticism can blow out the barely established flames, and not enough honesty can smother the momentum. Helpful criticism, on the other hand, can help the fire burn efficiently. But to radiate heat over a period of time, you must learn to handle the criticism wisely.

Seeing Enemies as a Sign of Change

How do you approach criticism wisely? The famous attorney, Clarence Darrow, was accused of jury tampering in Los Angeles in 1912. His eight-hour closing argument in his own defense led to his acquittal. In the midst of his self-defense he described his awareness that he was on trial, to a large extent, because of his unpopularity with certain people. Darrow told the jurors, "If you haven't made three or four enemies, gentlemen, you have lived a very weak and useless life. A man who can go through life as far as you twelve men have gone, and not make three or four enemies, is not worthwhile." His words can aptly be applied to anyone whose momentum is being challenged by criticism.

Nehemiah, like Hezekiah, was a man of God who used the power of momentum for the benefit of God's people. He helped the people of Jerusalem do something great—rebuild the protective city walls of Jerusalem. His ability to create and sustain significant momentum empowered the people to accomplish their goals. Not surprisingly, Nehemiah had enemies; anyone who stirs that kind of momentum in people can expect to have enemies. Nehemiah's two most prominent enemies were named Sanballat and Tobiah.

> Now when Sanballat heard that we were building the wall,
> he was angry and greatly enraged, and he mocked the Jews…
> Tobiah the Ammonite was beside him, and he said, "That
> stone wall they are building–any fox going up on it would
> break it down!" (Neh. 4:1, 3)

By the time the Israelites were well on their way to completing the walls of Jerusalem, a third enemy–Geshem–had joined the group. Geshem spread rumors that Nehemiah had a personal agenda. Geshem claimed that Nehemiah was only rebuilding the walls so he could become the king of Jerusalem (Neh. 6). Nehemiah refused to let these enemies extinguish the momentum as the people responded to God's call to rebuild the walls. When his enemies invited him to meet and discuss the rumors, he refused to attend their gathering. "I am doing a great work and I cannot come down. Why should the work stop while I leave it to come down to you?" (Neh. 6:3).

Nehemiah knew he needed to stay on target. He couldn't let the attacks of his enemies distract him. However, his enemies were not the only ones criticizing Nehemiah; some of his faithful workers also criticized him. Nehemiah confronted a dilemma that faces all leaders. How do you sift through the criticism, whatever its source, and decide what is legitimate and worthy of your attention? In other words, how do you learn to recognize and use legitimate criticism?

When to Listen to and Learn from Critics

The common reaction of most people is to go on the defensive when attacked. Leaders are no different. In anger and frustration, they tend to hear criticism as an attempt to halt their momentum. Nehemiah was no exception. Yet he quickly learned to discern the difference between the criticism coming from his enemies and the criticism coming from his counselors. The intentions of these two groups were very different. His enemies wanted to shut the project down, whereas his supporters wanted to refine the specifics of the plan to reach the goal.

In his book on Nehemiah, *Visioneering,* Andy Stanley points out that Nehemiah recognized that valid criticism could help a leader revise and improve his plan.[1] It helped him see the difference between the overall vision and the specific plans for implementing that vision. The vision was the call of God to rebuild the walls. The plans included the specific ways of delegating the financial and labor resources. Nehemiah saw how important it is to separate God's vision from our

---

[1]Andy Stanley, *Visioneering* (Sisters, Oreg.: Multnomah, 1999).

human plans. The vision was set, but he could allocate his resources in various ways to fulfill the call of God. In fact, Nehemiah willingly adapted the plans for implementation in response to legitimate criticism while remaining true to God's vision.

Unlike Nehemiah, we sometimes confuse our implementation plans with God's vision. If we believe our specific plans are of divine origin, then we tend to think our critics must be going against God's will. How dare they question our plans? But effective leaders learn to be flexible with their implementation plans. In so doing, they can respond to loyal critics in constructive ways while simultaneously resisting the attempts of their enemies to halt all progress.

Sanballat and Tobiah wanted to stop Nehemiah and the Jews from accomplishing their goals and threatened an attack to do this. When some of Nehemiah's people heard of the intended attacks, they criticized Nehemiah's plans to continue building without providing sufficient protection for the workers. His workers supported the goal, but they had serious concerns about personal danger as well as the failure of the entire project. They were genuinely afraid and asked that Nehemiah reconsider how the work was being done.

> But Judah said, "The strength of the burden bearers is failing, and there is too much rubbish so that we are unable to work on the wall." And our enemies said, "They will not know or see anything before we come upon them and kill them and stop the work." When the Jews who lived near them came, they said to us ten times, "From all the places where they live they will come up against us." (Neh. 4:10–12)

Leaders experience extreme difficulty in discerning the difference between helpful criticism intended to assist them in sharpening their plans and hurtful criticism intended to stop them. When his supporters asked him to take seriously the threat of an attack, Nehemiah could have discounted them as being nothing more than troublemakers. In his frustration and defensiveness, he might have lumped their criticism together with the criticism of those who were against the project. He might have refused to meet with them just as he refused to meet with his enemies. If he had, he would have missed out on some valuable input—criticism from people who shared his vision and supported him.

Finding Prophets among the Critics

How do we celebrate the fact that God provides us with helpful critics? Perhaps a good place to begin is to think of helpful critics as "prophets" and those with destructive criticism as "enemies." The next step is to develop the discernment for separating the prophets from the enemies. As a leader, you need to listen to and honor the prophets while combating the destructive criticism of your enemies.

This is what Nehemiah did. He realized that some of his critics' concerns were legitimate, so he adjusted his plans for the building of the walls. The prophetic voices wanted God's vision for Jerusalem as much as he did; they simply had concerns about how Nehemiah was proceeding. In response to these concerns, Nehemiah decided to set up extra guards and have the construction workers carry weapons. He created a trumpet signal to inform the workers of an attack. Thus, the work went forward, but it was based on plans that had been adjusted in response to the legitimate concerns for workers' safety.

Helping Prophets Be Prophetic

So the criticism of God's prophets can be a very important part of carrying on God's work effectively. However, prophets must be sensitive to the leader if their criticism is to be helpful and accelerate momentum. It isn't easy for prophets to figure out how to express their concerns in a way that contributes to a positive feed-forward, rather than a reactionary, culture. How can prophets help leaders hear their concerns so that the leaders will be willing to adjust plans for the benefit of the whole group? How, in other words, can you create a church culture in which prophets and leaders use criticism to work together effectively to discern God's will and create and sustain momentum? I believe the following five principles are a useful guide. Adopt these principles if you are a senior pastor, and teach them to your prophets and other leaders in your church so that they become an integral part of your church culture.

Be sensitive to the importance of timing.

One of our very active church members had the habit of catching me between Sunday worship services to express a concern. I let my defensiveness grow as time after time I found myself feeling ambushed by her criticisms. While her concerns were often legitimate, the timing was awful. Distracted by the demands of a busy Sunday preaching schedule, I found myself occasionally reacting more out of frustration than discernment. I mentally started to label her as a troublemaker, although this was not her intention. Her concerns were legitimate and often helpful. Her problem was timing.

If a prophet wants to offer helpful feedback to a leader without inflicting damage on the entire congregation, the prophet needs first to determine whether it's a good or a bad time to talk. It may be as simple as asking, "Is this a good time to talk, or would you prefer I call later at the office?"

In any case, pastors and prophets shouldn't hesitate to let one another know when it isn't a good time to discuss an issue. Susanna Wesley, mother of Charles and John Wesley, who founded the Methodist movement, used to pause in the midst of her busy day and simply lift her apron over her head to stop and pray. The older children in the family knew it was time to quietly take the younger children out of the room to give her a few moments to collect her thoughts. When she felt approachable again, she simply dropped her apron and continued her day. You may not have an apron to throw over your head, but sometimes just a look or a brief word is sufficient to let the other person know that the timing is not right.

Try to know a person's state of mind when you approach him or her with a concern.

This is related to sensitivity of timing, but it is more than just awareness of it's not being a good time because of an immediate situation. It can be a bad time for criticism because the other person is stressed or struggling with some longer-term matters. Most leaders, when they feel significant stress threatening momentum, tend to shut down temporarily at any criticism. The mind goes into shock. Just as the body goes into a temporary shutdown in the midst of a serious physical crisis, emotions can also go into shock. Knowing that this tends to happen, the wise prophet will recognize the symptoms of significant stress and save feedback for a better time. As Henry David Thoreau wrote, "It takes two to speak the truth—one to speak, and another to hear."

Some prophets in my life have helped me learn to identify when I am feeling fragile and when my momentum is flagging. These prophets insist that I regulate my intake of information so that I have balance in my life between affirmation and criticism. When recently have you as a leader openly asked for affirmation and admitted feeling fragile?

I trim our hedges at home when I feel fragile. My wife recognizes that I am feeling attacked when I come home, immediately get out the trimmers, and head for the hedges. She is ready for what happens next. I finish trimming a section of the hedges and call her outside to examine my work. In the early days I had to clarify what I wanted. "Okay, I trimmed the hedges and I need an ooooh, ahhhh!" And she'd respond "Wow, that looks really good!"

Now she knows the routine so well that I don't even verbalize my need for affirmation. She walks outside as I am winding down from an hour of sweaty outside work and celebrates how good the yard looks. She doesn't mention the missed branch. She waits a couple of days to point this out. For the moment, she knows that I am asking for affirmation, not criticism. Criticism at the wrong time can kill momentum and end a project.

As I developed this skill of balancing criticism at work with affirmation at home, I refined my abilities to be just as honest with staff and close friends as I work on sermons. I prepare my message a few weeks before I preach it so that I can print the rough draft and give it to a handful of people for their feedback and refinement. As a result, I seldom preach a sermon as originally written. Usually, I am open to immediate suggestions. However, occasionally when I am feeling tender for some reason, I know that further criticism may kill my fragile momentum. So I sometimes have asked my assistant to read but not critique the first draft of my sermon. I'll say something like, "Here is a masterpiece. I need you to tell me that it is the best piece of literature you have ever read. Assure me that Shakespeare would be jealous that he never put such amazing thoughts into English prose." She chuckles and inevitably enters my office later that day with very complimentary words. A few days later, however, after she checks out whether I am ready for helpful suggestions, she may offer some thoughtful ways to refine and improve it.

For that matter, my assistant reads my feelings rather well and guides me as to when she should pass on the criticisms that inevitably come in the mail. She occasionally asks, "Before you go through the mail, I need to ask, is this a good time to handle criticism?" She will volunteer to remove something that is critical if she recognizes that I don't need it right them. Sometimes I am ready to handle it. Other times I tell her to hold it for a better time. She is aware that her timing of passing on criticisms can affect my momentum.

Remind one another regularly that you are on the same side.

Our junior high leader a few months ago asked our adult choir director if he could please keep the instrumentalists from rehearsing in the choir room during the junior high Sunday school class. Of course, having the junior high room right next to the main choir room means there are bound to be moments when youth noise affects the choir and vice versa. For the most part the relationships have been understanding and supportive. But when the instrumentalists started rehearsing and warming up during the junior high class, the youth leaders realized this was a distraction that was hurting their ministry. The junior high leaders reminded the choir director they were on the same team with him and wanted both programs to be successful. They explained that during key moments when they were leading the youth into quiet reflection and prayer, instrumental warming up was particularly distracting to the junior high students. The communication was respectful and received well. It was clear that the youth leaders and the choir director (a former youth leader himself) were on the same team.

Unfortunately, as I listen to fellow pastors, such healthy interactions are not the norm in many churches. Groups within the church can easily turn against other groups and make it feel like battles between ministries. It can easily turn into *us* against *them* kinds of communications. A fellow pastor shared his frustration with just such a situation in his church.

A prayer group in his church was stirring up trouble. They felt the church needed an additional associate pastor on staff. When it was explained that the budget was tight and the church had no salary for that position, they immediately started studying the budget line by line. Pretty soon their prayer agenda to get another pastor turned into a crusade to show how unspiritual other ministries in the church were and why their budgets should be cut to make room for the new pastor. For instance, they criticized the line in the budget that for paid section leaders in the traditional adult choir. Rather than affirm that they were all on the same team and try to understand the needs of different styles of music in churches, they gave off signals that they considered themselves more spiritual because their contemporary service used an all-volunteer choir and did not pay any section leaders. It quickly deteriorated into a classic *us*-against-*them* worship war.

The pastor shared with me that he was exhausted as he tried to keep his people from tearing the fabric of the church with this unhealthy competitive spirituality. It isn't easy being the leader whose job is to call the whole congregation to remain united for the overall vision! We need to remind our people that we are all on the same team—the Lord's team. Help them to not assume the other person already knows that. Make it clear often in the midst of the conversation.

Treat all anonymous communications for what they are—messages that should be ignored and discarded.

Of course, this principle assumes that leaders are approachable, that offering a criticism will be accepted as an offer of help. Even so, some pastors may prefer to carefully consider such communications. My advice, however, is to tell your church secretary or administrative assistant to protect your momentum and energy for the benefit of the congregation. Here is what I would say to the person who opens my mail: "When you come across a letter, always make sure it is signed. Don't read the contents; just make sure it is signed. If the letter is unsigned, tear it up and throw it in the trash."

Many pastors don't have the protection of an administrative assistant or even a church secretary. The anonymous note shows up on the desk Monday morning. All it has on the outside is the pastor's first name. The pastor innocently opens it and then gets an arrow to the heart. What do you do?

I would urge you to accept the principle that an anonymous letter is never of God. It's always of the devil. I am convinced of this. When the Holy Spirit convicts us of something we need to change, God's Spirit always invites us into dialogue and gives us a chance to interact and clarify. Prophets don't send anonymous notes; dysfunctional people do. I have learned to say two things out loud as I toss the letter in the trash. "Get behind me Satan!" and "This is from a dysfunctional person who is so out of step with our congregation he or she doesn't even know how to dialogue respectfully." Then toss it and move on.

I recently received a note that made me laugh out loud. My assistant passed it on because it was signed with the initial *J*. She figured it was someone I knew well but realized it was critical. When she checked to see if it was a good time for me to receive something critical, I told her I was ready to handle legitimate criticism. At first I tried to figure out what friend whose name began with *J* was so upset with me. It took my assistant and me a few minutes to even figure out what the letter was addressing. It turned out to be an indirect complaint about the decision of our congregation to hire a new executive pastor. We eventually pieced together that the person writing the letter meant the initial *J* to represent the signature of Jesus. Can you imagine? Someone is so dysfunctional that he thinks he speaks for Jesus! Church leader, it's important to remember that your anonymous letter writer is just as dysfunctional. Don't let the devil steal your momentum.

View criticism as an essential part of what we might call a "feed-forward" process.

The challenge is for leaders to create a culture in which prophets are appreciated and feedback becomes feed-forward. Prophets often feel out of step, as if they are swimming upstream against the tide of momentum. They may feel that the leader has all of the power and is pushing the congregation in one way or another and that they are powerless to change the direction even the slightest little bit.

God sensitized me to the feelings of prophetic dissenters a few years ago when three elders on our board became concerned about the fast pace with which our church was moving toward a major capital campaign. In the excitement of our growing crowds, the overwhelming majority of the elders wanted to press forward and use the accelerating momentum to expand our facilities.

Twenty-one of the elders were ready to vote for beginning the financial campaign immediately and moving ahead toward construction. I could have pushed forward with a vote of twenty-one to three. Instead, I prayed about the matter. In my devotional time the Lord spoke to me through the passage in Daniel 3 in which Shadrach, Meshach, and Abednego withstood the power of King Nebuchadnezzar. As I reread this portion of scripture, I asked if any part of it applied to our situation. Then it hit me. Those three elders saw me as having the power and momentum on my side. And they felt like the three Israelites, doing what was unpopular by standing up to the king. They believed they were speaking prophetically to the one with power in this situation—me.

As I humbled myself before the Lord and prayed for help to bring our entire board of elders together, I realized that the three elders genuinely wanted the best for our church. They were not trying to stop the momentum of our growth but wanted to help refine the plans for construction as we moved forward. I realized they were not giving feedback so much as feed-forward. Once we saw the wisdom of their concerns and adjusted the plans, these same three elders became strong supporters of the construction. One even served on the capital campaign committee.

A positive-momentum church culture requires an atmosphere in which feedback is really feed-forward, so that you can refine the plans for the future. If leaders and prophets do not create a feed-forward culture, then most institutions will tend to be like the community in the children's story of *The Emperor's New Clothes*. Nobody wants to tell the truth to the leader, even though many can see the potential problems.

Feedback becomes feed-forward when we appreciate that our human implementation plans are not the same as God's vision. Thus, there is room for prophets to help leaders refine the plans. Feed-forward frees us to be flexible. We make better momentum choices when each person's ego is set aside to listen to one another. Feed-forward recognizes that prophets and leaders are on the same team.

Shake off the fiery arrows of dysfunctional prophets.

Of course, learning these skills will take time for you and your prophets to develop. In the meantime, it is inevitable that you will take hurtful arrows from a dysfunctional prophet whose timing is horrendous and agenda is personal. How do you shake it off?

I recently took a cheap shot from a former deacon. Just minutes before the start of the service, she approached me with fire in her eyes, got in my face, and angrily blurted out, "I just heard that you blocked _____'s nomination to leadership! How could you?!" With that she stomped away. Feeling seriously misunderstood, I hastily tried to explain the situation, but it was clear she was in no mood to listen. She seemed to have no awareness of my schedule. Even though I was preaching in a few minutes, she was angry and wanted to lash out at me.

As I turned to head into the service, I realized my body was pumping with adrenaline. My body was fired up for "fight or flight," and if anyone had said the wrong thing just then, it is likely my reaction would have been to fight! What to do?

I paused at the back of the sanctuary as the congregation began worship that morning without me. Staying at the back, I found a member of our prayer team and asked her to pray for me; then it was time to shake it off–literally. I needed to get the pumped-up hormones flushed out of my system so my brain could function again. Remaining at the back so the worship team knew I was there, I shook out my hands and wrists. I rotated my shoulders and neck. I bent over and stretched my back muscles and flexed my thighs and calves. I paced a couple times across the back of the sanctuary and rubbed the back of my neck to stop the incipient stress headache brought on by tight neck muscles. Like Jesus, who responded to Peter, "Get behind me Satan," I had to refocus on God's will for me that day, preaching God's word to God's people. Shaking off the fiery arrows required me to deal with the actual physicality of feeling attacked.

Fortunately, after a few minutes to refocus, by the time I went forward and preached that service I was back in the groove of ministry. My executive pastor, helping with the service that morning, told me later that he had no idea anything had happened.

Listening to Our Prophets to Build Momentum

Nehemiah's prophets helped him identify a number of legitimate concerns that needed to be changed for Jerusalem to get back on her feet. Even as he completed the specific goal of rebuilding the walls, he continued listening to his prophets and ended up shifting some economic policies in order to restore the trust of the people (Neh. 5). He learned from his critics that he needed to institute Sabbath practices to sustain the spiritual momentum of the people (Neh. 13). Withstanding his enemies did not mean he should stop listening to his prophets.

We need to listen to our prophets. It is my experience that the Holy Spirit often answers our prayers and guides us by speaking to us through the counsel of trusted friends (who are also prophets in our lives). As we open our hearts to listen for God's whisper, friends show up without realizing that their words are God's prophetic warning or encouragement.

Years ago, I was in the interview stage with a church in the Northwest. The committee was interested in having me become their pastor. It was a large, successful congregation with much that I found exciting. However, I didn't have peace as I prayed about it. Kathy and I spent much of our spring vacation praying and talking about this possibility. Our teenage children were included in the conversation. But after much prayer and conversation, we still lacked any sense of clarity as to whether or not I should pursue the position. It looked so good–a larger church, with a larger salary and more responsibilities. It felt like a perfect match for my gifts, interests, and skills. Yet I still lacked a clear sense of call from God.

Then the answer came in a surprising way. One day a relatively new member of our church arrived at my office and asked if he could talk. He sat down and told me that he felt that the Lord wanted him to come make himself better known to me. He decided to tell me his story.

As a young man, he had joined a company that had promoted him to new responsibilities within the same general locality. By the time he was in his thirties, he was in charge of significant portions of the company's sales. The promotions and bonuses kept coming. Life was good. His family was doing well. Then he got the chance of a lifetime. The company offered him his dream promotion. He was placed in charge of their entire west-coast operations. The salary was amazing. As far as his professional life was concerned, he had "made it."

At this point in his story, he paused and reflected before continuing. "Bruce, I had not considered what that move would do to our family. It nearly destroyed our daughters. They got into the wrong crowd and developed some unhealthy behaviors." He shared few details, but made it clear that the change had been very costly to his family. He finished his story with these words, "If I had it to do over again, I would give up that last promotion and make my family a priority over a successful career."

When he stood to leave, he commented, "I don't really know why I stopped by to tell you this today. Who knows? Maybe someday you'll get an offer that looks really good at first, but I advise you to always count the cost to your family." When he left, I called Kathy and told her what had just happened. We agreed it was the Holy Spirit's answer to our prayers, and within a day I had pulled my name from consideration. The Lord showed us a few months later that it was the right decision.

Momentum and Self-criticism

One final point needs to be made about criticism. Not all of it comes from others. Indeed, you may be your own worst critic. Just as you learn to differentiate the voices of the prophetic critics from those of the enemies, you need to learn to distinguish the voice of the Holy Spirit from other internal distracting voices in your personal life. In the same way that Nehemiah's enemies spread rumors to stir up a general sense of fear, so may internal voices stir up fear in your personal life. But God "did not give us a spirit of cowardice, but rather a spirit of power and of love and of self-discipline" (2 Tim. 1:7). Here's a fairly simple litmus test to determine whether an internal voice is from God or not: If it makes you fearful but gives you no specific insights for correction, it is not from God. If it makes you feel like a victim who can't change, it is not from God.

Internal voices often come out of childhood memories–the criticism of a parent, the voices of playmates who made fun of us, the harsh words of overly competitive coaches, or hurtful criticisms from adults in authority. Although such voices spread feelings of hopelessness and helplessness, the Holy Spirit speaks with a very different message. He not only directs us to repent from specific sins but also reminds us that we can change with God's intervention. God's voice helps us feel empowered because we realize the situation is not hopeless. God reveals to us options we had not recognized. We discover that we can do all things through Christ our Lord.

The Holy Spirit corrects us by reminding us that we can become more fully the person God intends us to be. The prophetic voice of God's Spirit pinpoints our sin rather than leaving us with a vague, uncertain malaise. We come away from a genuine encounter with

God feeling challenged and cleansed and wanting to move forward. God's correction is actually a compliment because we realize that God has exciting, hopeful plans for our future (Jer. 29:11). In other words, God gives us feed-forward instead of feedback.

CHAPTER 5

Nehemiah Aligns the Reward System

Phoenix was cooking that afternoon. As the airline captain announced that the temperature in Phoenix was 105, the passengers responded with a united moan. The driver who picked me up at the airport commented that it was an unusual heat wave for so early in the year. His banter was friendly, but his air conditioner was not keeping up with the temperatures radiating off the highway. I was not looking forward to the next few days.

I serve on the board of trustees at Cook College and Theological School—a Native American institution historically related to the Presbyterians. I've been to the campus dozens of times over the years, and the place has always seemed to be in a sorry condition. The buildings have been allowed to deteriorate as the finances have limped along. The air conditioning in the dorm rooms doesn't usually work. To be honest, the campus is pretty seedy.

But as we drove onto the campus that day, I was amazed at the change. The buildings sported fresh paint. New cactus gardens and desert trees spruced up the campus. The grassy areas were green and manicured. I did a double take. Was this the same school where I have taught, written a few textbooks, and now serve on the board? The transformation was amazing.

After dropping my bags off in a dorm room that was nicely air conditioned, I went to dinner where I heard a story of transformation. The college's interim president shifted the culture on campus by rewarding new things. He wanders into various offices to give frequent affirmations. The dean of the theological school commented that the new interim president gives regular "atta-boys." When the interim president decided the school needed to look nicer so that it could better appeal to contributors and recruit more students, he decided to pay attention to the grounds crew. It's working. The atmosphere among faculty and students is the most upbeat I have seen in twenty years of relating to this school.

That interim president has shifted the school's rewards system. He is modeling what he wants for the rest of the faculty and staff. He rewards progress toward his goals with his affirmations.

Rewards Reinforce Momentum

What does your church reward? Whatever you reward will grow. It's like opening the air valves of the woodstove after adding more wood to the fire. The flames need to engulf the added wood. If you give the fire more oxygen, the flames will spread. In a similar way, when you've put into place plans and actions to lead your congregation in a new direction, you need to find ways to reinforce the momentum.

Nehemiah had to do this after enemies nearly sabotaged his work of restoration. Upon the completion of the walls, Nehemiah departed Jerusalem and returned to his duties with the king in the foreign palace. During his absence some of those in charge of the Jerusalem temple invited Tobiah, one of the enemies who had tried to stop the building of the walls, back into favor. Nehemiah quickly discovered that the momentum of the construction period already was waning.

Tobiah had taken over one of the temple storage rooms, and attitudes were reverting to their former state. Nehemiah took action. He had Tobiah's belongings removed from the temple. He then worked at clarifying their new cultural values and aligning everything to them (Neh. 13). Nehemiah realized that the reward system needed to line up with the desired culture.

Nehemiah appreciated the fact that institutional systems naturally tend to revert to their former inertia. If you wish to reinforce a group's new momentum direction, you must establish new institutional rewards to maintain that direction. He understood that not rewarding the faithful priests would undercut the momentum of regular, vibrant worship. He discovered that many of the singers and Levites had not been paid their salaries and so had returned to laboring in the fields.

In frustration, Nehemiah confronted Jerusalem's leaders with their failure to maintain the new direction. He challenged them: "Why is the house of God forsaken?" (Neh. 13:11).

Inconsistent Rewards Undercut Momentum

As Nehemiah discovered, inconsistency in the reward system undercuts momentum. Since institutions tend naturally to revert back to the comfortable inertia of the past, you must be intentional in creating a reward system that reinforces your new direction. This is particularly true in churches.

From the moment I arrived in my current church, I made it clear that my highest priority was developing healthy relationships as a core value of our congregational culture. I held up the vision of cooperation, trust, and teamwork. I maintained that if we stopped fighting turf battles and instead took care of each other, positive momentum would drive our church forward.

Clearly, this was not the way things worked when I arrived. I inherited a competitive culture with a reward system in place that maintained that culture. Instead of a group of cooperative servant-leaders, the staff was an assemblage of competitive individuals. Staff members talked behind their colleagues' backs. Some of them refused to openly discuss their disagreements; rather they passively resisted the other's hopes and dreams. Moreover, I discovered that parts of the institutional system actually rewarded this uncooperative, competitive behavior.

For instance, our annual staff evaluation system, taken from a corporate competitive approach, encouraged staff to compete against each other for raises. Whatever lip service I gave to teamwork and cooperation, the basic salary system was rewarding competition between ministries. Is it any surprise that our church often ran as a loose coalition of separate ministries? You were rewarded financially for *not* helping other ministries to be successful.

Modeling the Rewards System

Where do you start when you want to shift your culture and reward new priorities? Nehemiah modeled his new priorities. He not only religiously revered the Sabbath as a holy day, but he also insisted that the gates of the city be locked during the Sabbath so there could be no trade on that holy day (Neh. 13:15–22).

Taking a page from Nehemiah, I realized that our church needed someone to model the desired behavior. Modeling was necessary both to change the culture and to enable a new reward system to be effective (people had to see the kind of behavior that was going to be rewarded). And who better to model the desired behavior than I? I therefore determined to *show* the staff the kind of behavior I hoped would become the norm. I discovered that what *I* modeled was more effective in changing the culture than all my words about cooperation at staff meetings.

One step I took was to volunteer to do dishes in the church kitchen. I've mentioned before how my doing dishes after a church supper helped set a new direction in our church values. Here's why. Over the years, many in our "country club" church had developed the notion that the paid custodians and kitchen workers were the only ones who should move tables and chairs, set up coffee, clean the dishes, and do the menial tasks. When people saw their "C.E.O." engaged in these tasks, it sent shock waves through the congregational culture. As one of the surprised volunteers said, "The head of staff pastor washing dishes? Let me put my teeth back in my mouth!"

My modeling the example of the servant-leader in this way led to change in the church's culture. Other relatively small actions added to the change. During construction on our sanctuary, for example, it was necessary to regularly turn the fellowship hall into a worship center and back again within a short period of time. Initially, I enlisted members of my Wednesday-evening Bible study to join me in readying the room for Thursday-morning events. Soon others joined us.

I learned that what I start catches the attention of others. If I am moving chairs, congregation members want to help me. We laugh and talk as we work side by side. When I help a young family find the nursery in between services, someone takes over for me and leads the visitors to the location. If I move chairs on and off the platform between different style services, others quickly move in to help.

Pastor, your people enjoy spending time with you. What you do, they will usually join in doing simply to be near you. Do you want to recruit volunteers to build a Habitat for Humanity home? Show up every so often with your hammer, and watch your volunteerism increase exponentially. Go on a mission trip, and watch how many in the congregation show a new interest in participating in missions.

What the leader models is what the people will do. People become servant-leaders only when they see it modeled at the top of the organization. It's now a common sight to see church members moving chairs, cleaning tables, and helping transform a room from one activity to the next. Our congregational culture has changed!

Informal and Institutional Rewards Solidify Culture Changes

Not only does the leader model what we want, but we also reward it through informal means. When I pause to give a word of appreciation to the volunteers who come in on Saturday morning to answer our phones, it is like an emotional deposit into their hearts. A personal note of thanks that tells the men's group how much I appreciate their helping move the piano for the concert is gold. I don't do it enough, but I try to send personal notes to affirm individuals as I see them participating around our congregation. I have found that what feels small and inadequate from my perspective sometimes turns out to be prized by those receiving them.

Once the people buy into the new culture, however, the institutional as well as informal reward system must be reworked to sustain it. Eventually our desire to maintain positive momentum toward healthy relationships meant we had to change the salary structure and the system of annual performance evaluations. We had to shift some job descriptions to play to people's strengths as well as create better teamwork. We moved offices, forcing people who had been emotionally distant to work in closer proximity until the relationships grew more cooperative. Alignment of the rewards to reinforce our priority of healthy relationships is ongoing. It takes constant vigilance to avoid reverting to previous ingrained habits.

Refusing Rewards for Problem People

Hopefully, your reward systems will cultivate a church where people work together in healthy ways. But some people are impervious to such a system. For example, what do you do with an employee who steadfastly resists the changed culture? In our case, what do you do with someone who acts in ways that subvert the servant-leader culture? We faced such a situation some years ago. While every organization has occasional employee problems, church leaders are notorious for failing to confront head-on problems with staff and key congregational leaders. We try to practice forgiveness as Jesus taught us to do. And then we get into trouble because we misunderstand what it means to forgive.

Forgiveness does not mean we allow an employee or key volunteer to undercut our momentum by continuing to be out of alignment with the culture. Forgiveness does not mean we ignore or justify destructive behavior. Forgiveness does not mean that we say nothing to people who do not think they need to be forgiven, or who do not even realize there is an issue. Such efforts to practice forgiveness miss the point and are one of the easiest ways to kill a church's momentum.

Here's what happened with our employee. As the culture of our congregation began to change, a group of the staff asked for a meeting to discuss our options regarding one of their colleagues who was clearly out of alignment with the changes. Some of his recent behavior was unacceptable to them. What would it mean to forgive him? How many times should we allow him to keep doing the same destructive things? Were we unintentionally enabling him to subvert the amazing changes in our congregation? The employee's supervisor listened to fellow staff as they described their frustrations with this colleague. He was not working well with the rest of the team. His behavior was contrary to our emphasis on the importance of healthy relationships, and those who worked alongside him were frustrated by his lack of care and concern. Worse, he was unresponsive to all efforts to get him to alter his behavior.

To sustain the momentum of positive change, we had to confront this problem. I moderated the staff meeting where we discussed this person's behavior. There were uncomfortable moments, of course. However, by the end of the meeting it was clear that the supervisor needed to fire the employee for the sake of our teamwork culture. The pain of this decision was offset for me by the realization that the values driving our culture of cooperation had not only taken hold, but were now running the institution.

As the commitment to develop healthy relationships spread from the staff to increasingly larger segments of the congregation, difficult decisions became easier to make. In fairly short order, the staff had led the board and elders to make the same commitment—sparking even greater momentum. For instance, when a zealous board member passionately defended a particular ministry area at the expense of another area, staff members from both areas were quick to defend each other. Thankfully, we have watched the entire culture of our church shift to higher trust relationships not only because our leaders modeled this behavior but also because the institutional support systems were aligned to sustain that momentum direction.

In other words, just as you cannot allow a staff member to subvert the church's culture in the name of "forgiveness," neither can you allow people to do terrible things to each other. You cannot let people engage in and justify hurtful, unhealthy interactions. You cannot allow a few strong-willed people to have veto power over the rest. In short, you cannot reward people for counterproductive or destructive kinds of behavior. To do so is a sure way to douse the fire of momentum.

Stifling Momentum through Wrong Rewards

Consider how we reward the wrong things around our churches. The primary reward system in churches is the giving of attention, recognition, and time. Show me where the pastor and elected church leadership spend the majority of their time, and I can predict where their church momentum is headed.

Many churches use the majority of time in their board meetings to discuss how to respond to a particularly difficult personality. Church leaders often reward their dysfunctional members with attention. Too many pastors fall into the reactionary use of their time by running from one discontented member to another.

Here is a simple test to see what the pastor tends to reward. Picture this: the pastor returns to the office after lunch. On the desk are two notes. One note says an elder called to clarify how best to present a positive report to the board that evening. The other note says that one of the most needy, most demanding members insists on an immediate call. She is upset by the choice of hymns at last week's service and is threatening to withdraw her pledge. However, the pastor has only enough time to make one phone call before his next appointment. Which of these members does he call? If the pastor puts off the elder and responds to the demanding parishioner, then, that pastor will tend to be surrounded by needy, demanding parishioners. If the pastor calls the elder, that pastor likely serves a church where the leaders feel appreciated and share the work of the ministry.

What we reward grows. When church leaders reward chronic complainers with extra attention, it should not surprise them that they are repaid with more complainers. If, on the other hand, leaders reward the faithful, hard workers with affirmation and attention, more people will become active in the ministries of the church. If pastors rush to meet with persistently discontented church members at the expense of spending time with the active members who faithfully serve day in and day out, it ought not to surprise us when the church grows increasingly dysfunctional.

Growing Momentum by Rewarding Ourselves

The same is true in our personal lives. What we reward grows. I have known people who remain crisis-driven because they unintentionally reward themselves for being stressed and busy at the expense of efficiency. They validate their importance by how rushed they feel. It doesn't have to be this way.

Dr. Margie Blanchard coached our staff last year about the use of our time as leaders. She reminded us that if you ask an elementary school child what he enjoys most at school, the answer will be "recess." Why? Because it is the only moment in the typical daily school schedule when the child has control over his or her time. If she wants to play on the monkey bars, she can. If he wants to play ball, he can. Margie challenged our staff to take control of our own schedules and reward ourselves for doing what will maintain momentum as we work to achieve our long-range goals.

Listening to Dr. Blanchard, I realized that I had gradually taken on more and more of the administrative tasks it takes to run our large church. I was attending too many meetings at the expense of my study and sermon preparation time. I needed to do more than review my priorities and make promises to do better. I needed to create a new reward system that reinforces a better schedule.

How often do we make the mistake of maintaining the same reward system while remaining frustrated by the results? If we want different results, we have to change the rewards. One caveat here: Inertia is comfortable and thus can feel like a reward. So we often cling to the old and comfortable. However, in the process we settle for less, and things stay the same. Change requires that, like Hezekiah, we do things differently and also demands that, like Nehemiah, we reinforce what is done by changing the rewards.

Developing Multiple Reward Systems

I've talked about rewards in terms of giving people attention, recognition, and time. But there are many ways to reward! It will be well worth your time to think about effective ways you can reward those with whom you work. A few years ago, our staff instituted a simple system of tangible rewards to help us affirm and appreciate each other. Our office manager bought some gift certificates to various local stores and restaurants. We then encouraged supervisors to look for positive behaviors that reinforced our new culture. They were instructed to reward the person not only with a compliment but also with a gift certificate. It was fun when we would work together to pick out the best gift certificate for the person we wanted to acknowledge. "Let's give Dave a certificate to a home improvement store." "How about a certificate to the pet store for Anne?"

Once the supervisors got the hang of using these expressions of affirmation, we enlarged the practice so that staff members could reward any other staff member with a gift certificate. This system of rewards caught on; in fact, it was so successful we eventually had to give smaller gift certificates to express our appreciation for a job well done.

So use your imagination to come up with various ways to align your reward system with your culture. If you don't do this, you will always stand at the brink of reverting back. But if you do establish an appropriate reward system, you will have taken a significant step toward maintaining momentum.

CHAPTER 6

Nehemiah Celebrates with Musical Fireworks

I suppose air pollution laws eliminated the Christmas tree bonfires of the 1950s. It's too bad. Our children don't have any memories of the huge bonfires in early January that were a part of my growing up. For those unfamiliar with Christmas tree bonfires in January, let me describe them.

The twentieth century was a time of great transition in America. When our great-grandparents moved from the rural farm life of their childhoods to the city life of industrial America, they brought with them a few remnants of the old life. For instance, every year in January in Tucson people from our newly developed neighborhoods brought their dead, dried Christmas trees to an empty lot near the local elementary school to join in an evening bonfire. It was a practical way to dispose of the old trees as well as to gather the neighborhood in a fun time for children to play around the edges and for adults to catch up on gossip. The winter bonfire brought our community together.

I think the fire department was in charge of the actual fire. What I remember was the sense of excitement just before the mound of trees went up in blazes. We usually had hundreds of dead trees. (My childhood memory tells me the tree stack must have been thirty feet high.) The crowd waited in anticipation. Were there speeches? I think so, but I wasn't paying attention. What stands out in my memory was the roar of the fire and the dancing of the flames. In some primal way the event symbolized another year off to a good start. Standing around the bonfire meant we would be there to support one another whatever the coming year might bring. Enjoying the heat radiating from the fire somehow symbolized the renewing of our relationships as neighbors. It was a celebration of tribal friendship.

Traditional Holiday Celebrations

In our churches we create similar celebrations for the holidays. Something holy and mysterious happens every Christmas Eve when the congregation passes the flame from candle to candle. The spreading of the candlelight reminds us that the light invades the darkness and the darkness will not win. Christmas is obviously a big celebration.

Most of our churches go all out for Christmas Eve services. These are the services not only to pass out candles but also for tympani and brass. We dim the lights for the candlelight and then bring up the crescendo of music and lights as we nearly shout the final words of the hymn "Joy to the World." Our churches are great at celebrations for Christmas.

Easter is the other big celebration for churches. I know of a church that prepares for its Easter sunrise service by having an all-night campfire vigil. Their tradition began in the days when they met in a rented facility but owned land for a future building. Years ago, a congregational leader came up with a suggestion to keep them hopeful and expectant about building their future sanctuary. They decided to gather the emerging congregation at the property designated for future development and have a Saturday night bonfire before Easter. Various families took turns tending the fire until Easter Sunday morning. Just before sunrise they added more wood to the fire and fanned it into flame. The sunrise service took place around the blazing fire.

Even though the tradition began years ago and they now have their sanctuary, members in this rural congregation still enjoy taking turns watching the fire from Saturday until the Easter sunrise service. It makes their Easter sunrise celebration special.

Celebrating to Reinforce New Values

Our churches know how to celebrate. When we walk into the sanctuary to discover the ushers handing out candles, we know something special is going to happen. If we spot extra musicians at the front of the sanctuary ready to accompany the singing, we know we are in for something special. But here is a question: How often and for what reasons do we celebrate?

Celebrations are the best way an entire congregation can reinforce their new values. Momentum toward a new direction requires not only that the leaders model the values and that the reward systems shift to reinforce the values, but also that the whole congregation celebrate the new direction. Special celebrations reinforce the values of the church culture. Unfortunately, many churches only celebrate Christmas and Easter, and have gone years without celebrating other events and accomplishments.

When was the last time you broke out the candles and brought in guest musicians other than on a Christmas Eve? When did you last decorate your fellowship hall with balloons and banners to celebrate a special offering or a successful mission trip? Have your youth put on a celebration service recently to tell their stories of what God is doing in their lives? When did you last celebrate an adult conversion as though you were joining the angels in their joyful dance at the repentance of a sinner? When did your congregation last meet a difficult goal and hold an old-fashioned ice cream social to celebrate its success?

Show me a church that only celebrates Christmas and Easter, and I'll show you a church that is stuck in inertia. Further, I'll show you a church that is threatened by complaints and unhealthy conflict. Celebration is the best way I know to be proactive and halt criticism and complaints before they get started. Nehemiah knew that the best defense against complaints is a good offense. He minimized the power of complainers by creating celebration events that reinforced the new culture he had worked to generate.

Nehemiah's Celebration

Nehemiah wanted to celebrate the completion of the walls of Jerusalem. Scholars agree that the dedication of the walls most likely occurred three months after the walls were completed. Why did they wait three months? The dedication service took incredible planning.

First, they planned a special musical service by gathering the Levites with their musical instruments. They had the musicians playing cymbals, lyres, and harps; and the singers gathered for special rehearsals ahead of time. They came in from the outlying areas to prepare for the big dedication ceremony. Music sounds different inside the walls of the city than out in the villages. The instrumentalists needed to rehearse to keep the singers walking on the walls on the same beat with the band in the middle of the city. Imagine a musical service in which the singers are moving away from one another around the city walls. It took rehearsal!

Next, the priests performed ceremonial cleansing services. They bathed according to special customs and changed their clothing. They performed hundreds of animal sacrifices to purify not only themselves but also the people who would be participating. They probably led special prayer services leading up to the day of dedication. Then, on the day of dedication, the priests robed up and prepared to march in the procession along the top of the walls.

Finally, Nehemiah gathered the political leaders to participate. "Then I brought the leaders of Judah up onto the wall, and appointed two great companies that gave thanks and went in procession" (Neh. 12:31). Once he had divided the leaders into two groups, he sent one group marching and singing to the right and the other group marching and singing to the left. Imagine the effect when the residents of the city not only listened to the music but also watched the parade of their leaders singing and marching along the newly completed walls. No wonder it took months to prepare for this great celebration. If Nehemiah had fireworks, I'm sure he would have used them as well.

When our congregation completed its $6 million expansion of the sanctuary and new youth complex, we took a page from Nehemiah. Our leaders took several months planning how to celebrate this accomplishment. The celebration weekend included balloons and banners across our campus. We showed a video of the history of our construction to remind us of what the old sanctuary was like before we tore it down and expanded it. We had an evening service that went two hours with testimonies of how participation in this process had grown people's faith and transformed their lives. We hosted local city dignitaries and neighbors in a ribbon-cutting ceremony/worship dedication service on Saturday morning. Saturday evening we surrounded the new facilities with people holding candles and then passed a flame from person to person all the way around the outside of our buildings. We concluded each Sunday morning worship service by offering tours of the new facilities. The fellowship hall was not only decorated, but included a spread of our chef's finest delicacies. In other words, we celebrated!

Celebrations Cut off Complaints

Celebrations not only move the entire congregation toward new values, they also subvert potential whining and complaining. How easy is it for someone who has attended such a weekend to continue whining about the color of the carpet? A person feels silly announcing to his friends that he doesn't like the selection of chandeliers when they have just sung a hymn accompanied with brass and drums and concluded the service with a standing ovation for the new facilities.

Of course, most of us are not in the midst of such dramatic and obvious construction. So how can we join Nehemiah in the proactive celebrations that reduce complaints and cement the new congregational culture we desire? We can do what the early Roman Christians did—borrow holidays.

Let's recall why we celebrate Christmas on December 25. It was not the actual date of Jesus' birth. We borrowed a pagan Roman holiday to help Christian families celebrate what we believe. The Romans celebrated shortly after the winter solstice that the sun was born afresh and the days had grown their darkest. If the shortest day was December 21, then by December 25 the people would realize that the days were growing ever so slowly longer. The light was coming into the world, and the sun was born. The Romans had a holiday to celebrate that light had once again beat back the darkness. Sun worshipers celebrated on December 25 that their god was born.

The early Christians borrowed this holiday to celebrate that Jesus is the true light of the world. His birth represents the light coming into the world with the darkness unable to resist it. Thus, the date of December 25 became an important celebration for Christians to remind themselves of the victory of light over darkness through Jesus' incarnation. Now, we who follow Jesus are to be light in the dark world.

Likewise, modern Easter has more in common with a Northern European tribal pagan holiday than with the ancient Passover. Our modern calendar ties Easter in with the spring vernal equinox, as opposed to the Jewish calendar. Christians borrowed someone else's holiday celebrations and turned them into a reinforcement of our own values. Rather than celebrate the spring fertility of new life in flowers and the fecundity of the fauna, we turned it into a celebration of Jesus' resurrection from death to life.

Borrowing and Creating Celebration Days

If the early Christians could do this, why can't we? Let's consider how we could create our own celebrations by borrowing holidays within our own culture. Some obvious holidays come to mind. How about creating Christian celebrations around Memorial Day or Independence Day?

For years I have fought valiantly to turn Pentecost into an important celebration. I have preached on the Bible story from Acts 2. I have emphasized to more than one congregation that the Day of Pentecost is not only the arrival of the Holy Spirit for all believers but also the birthday of the Christian church as an institution. I have encouraged worshipers to dress in red clothing to symbolize the flames of the Holy Spirit. We have decorated the fellowship hall and planned special parts of worship. But it is like pushing a huge boulder uphill. The fact is that our culture is already relaxing into summer vacations by early June. Because Pentecost almost always falls in early June, we are fighting a losing battle.

So why not tie in something special to Memorial Day weekend? In my two smaller ministries with worshiping congregations of less than two hundred, we developed a tradition of including an extended, special prayer time on Memorial Day weekend. We would invite congregation members to call out the names of loved ones they recalled on that weekend. In our mobile society I reminded the congregation that not all of us live near the gravesites of our loved ones, but we could still pause and remember. We have planned a church picnic and/or a special concert for an evening over Memorial Day weekend. Our current church has a family camp that weekend. Many families enjoy camping out and consider Memorial Day weekend the first good camping weekend. Why not play to that schedule?

In other words, instead of fighting the normal holiday schedule and trying to get people to engage in the early June date of Pentecost, we have found it easier to plan around the familiar holiday schedule that already exists in our society. The same is true when it comes to Labor Day.

Most churches plan their kickoff of the new Sunday school year in late August or early September. Why? This is because we coordinate our church schedule with the school schedules. In this case, so many families see Labor Day as the last chance to get away before settling into the fall school routine. So it seems silly to fight this natural seasonal event and try to commit our people to stay home with us and participate in a celebration of labor. We have found it is better to gear up a major celebration of the new Sunday school classes by bringing in the parent-teachers and commissioning them before the classes start. We can make the first week of the fall schedule a big kick-off celebration, using familiar football imagery from the season.

Not only can this be done using the seasonal national holidays, but it also works to tie in the church schedule with the local community events calendar. Our congregation in Arizona decided to create a church celebration to coincide with the local Western heritage weekend. The entire community geared up to remember the pioneers who first settled the old West. It was a weekend of history. The downtown was crowded with tourists. So our church decided to develop a "Western Sunday" celebration.

For our Western Sunday we rented a nearby camp. The worship service was styled after an old-fashioned revival tent meeting. We were surrounded with bales of hay and benches in an old barn. Decorations included saddles and six-guns. We encouraged the congregation to wear cowboy clothing. Each year I would welcome the congregation with a "Howdy!" Music was hand-clapping foot-stomping gospel. Each year I concluded my sermon to this traditional Presbyterian congregation with an un-Presbyterian altar call. Each year people raved about the celebration as helping them get back to their priorities. One year we used the camp setting to burn our mortgage and celebrate in the rustic setting how blessed we were to have completed a recent expansion.

What does your church celebrate? Some churches celebrate their Scottish heritage by parading their family tartans and including a time in the service for the pastor to pray and bless the tartans. Some congregations have special celebrations of their youth's baptisms or first communions. Some congregations celebrate special missions weekends when their missionaries guest preach and stir the congregation with wonderful stories of sacrifice and conversion happening in other cultures.

Our current congregation celebrated a new emphasis by having our first "Volunteer Recognition Weekend" last fall. We have decided that we want to reinforce to our congregation the expectation that everyone has gifts and abilities to share for the blessing of others. As our volunteerism shifts from the typical twenty-eighty rule (twenty percent of the congregation does eighty percent of the work), we have decided to honor and appreciate those who participate in volunteer ministries.

A team went to work to create a celebration that would reinforce the cultural value of volunteerism. That weekend we had decorations and balloons around our courtyard. We handed out a small flashlight gift to everyone with the name of the church and the explanation that we are all the light of the world. We took a moment in worship to applaud those who serve as volunteers in the various ministries. Lest any feel left out, we also took a moment for the entire congregation to stand in recognition that everybody benefits from the many hours of volunteerism that keep our church functioning. Refreshments in the fellowship hall were special that weekend.

The Significance of Celebration

Do such celebrations really matter? Listen to this story.

This last spring I wandered around giving appreciation to all the volunteers it takes to put on our Saturday Easter egg hunt for the community. With more than a hundred congregation members giving their time to bless the community and welcome families onto our church campus, I cannot pause very long with any one person. As I was greeting and giving lots of atta-boys, one of the volunteers asked if he could take a couple moments to tell me how much the church had come to mean to him.

He explained that he had just recently joined our church. He then told me why he decided to join. His first visit to our church was the volunteer recognition weekend. He watched as hundreds of people stood and were appreciated for their giving of time to help others. He was so impressed that our church has such an emphasis on participation and not simply attending that he told me he decided he wanted this to be his family's church. A few weeks later when the whole family moved into their home, he was excited to bring them to our congregation. Six months later he was already volunteering to help with the Easter egg hunt.

The celebrations can be small as well. They don't have to be big holiday extravaganzas. We can create small celebration events for our board meetings or staff. How about cookies and a festive environment once in a while for the group that volunteers to fold the bulletins on Fridays? Maybe we could celebrate with donuts and coffee those who count money for the church on Mondays.

I've mentioned that our whole staff has once-a-month breakfast gatherings. Each month we invite two staff members to pair up and decorate the room for the breakfast. The ones doing the decorating get to choose a theme and turn it into a mini-celebration. My turn to decorate this year fell during the month of March. A custodian and I were paired to decorate. We decided to focus on St. Patrick's Day. We told the story of the mission work of St. Patrick and then encouraged the staff at each table to talk about what it means to engage in mission today. Each table group was to give their centerpiece mug to the person at their table they wanted to honor for evangelistic and mission outreach across cultures. One table group celebrated the evangelism of Clara, a member of our kitchen staff who lives in the inner city and serves in her bilingual congregation.

Celebrations Create Growth

What we celebrate grows. If we want to shift our congregational culture, celebrate what we want. Years ago, I ran into a youth leader who now lives out of state but used to serve at our church. He told me his story. He recalled a morning he was working with our senior high youth program. He bounded into a staff meeting with the news that one of the young men in our high school group had received Jesus as his Lord and Savior. He expected affirmation and excitement. Instead, he received looks of apathy and barely a head nod. He commented, "Bruce, you wouldn't believe it. Nobody seemed to care. This young man's life was new in Christ, and they just wanted to keep running the church institution." It is no surprise that he was ready to move on to a church that would be more appreciative of his evangelistic passion.

Contrast that experience with a recent staff meeting. After Easter we took an entire staff meeting to celebrate how God had touched some lives in significant ways through our ministries over the past couple of months. We immediately celebrated that we had had more than twenty people fill out cards stating that they had come to faith in Jesus on Easter Sunday. Some of them were youth who had participated in the recent youth musical or had gone on the spring senior high mission trip to Mexico. Others were adults who had been around our church for a while and finally connected that Jesus offers them complete grace. Most of them were people we had been reaching out to through multiple ministries.

Was it the youth musical before Easter? Were they touched by the special Last Supper services or the "Mornings with the Master" series led by different pastors each morning in the chapel during Holy Week? Maybe it was the prayer group or a sermon. Maybe the head of our evangelism department's explanation after the Easter sermon finally helped them connect the dots and see God's design for their lives. We knew that it was not the result of any one person or ministry, but of our whole team. So how did we respond? The entire staff burst into applause and cheered. We were part of God's transforming the lives of twenty people! That is huge! It makes all our work worthwhile.

If your congregation hasn't had a celebration for a while, maybe it is time to start planning one. Momentum spreads when people enjoy what they are doing and receive affirmation for it. First, we need to decide what it is we want to appreciate and reward. When we celebrate, we steal the momentum from the whiners and complainers. The best defense is a good offense.

CHAPTER 7

Isaiah Learns about Dangerous Hot Coals

Every year in late August or early September my wife and I celebrate that our oldest son is alive and doing well. I mentioned earlier that when he was a junior in high school we feared that God was calling him home. What we took to be a tragedy at the time has become worthy of celebration. Moreover, it has taught me some important lessons about passing momentum from one ministry to another. Let me share his story.

One morning in late August, our son didn't wake up. Nate, who was sixteen at the time, had been battling a flu virus but thought he was feeling well enough to go to school the next day. When I went to awaken him that morning, I found him having seizures in the midst of a coma. He was in the grip of a sudden attack of meningeal encephalitis that would change his and our lives forever.

Nate went to sleep in August and didn't awaken until September. For a few days he remained in a coma under constant care of the doctors in the intensive care ward of the local hospital. Our congregation and community rallied to support us. We wouldn't have made it through those days without the safety net of their love and prayers. In the midst of this horrific experience we realized why the Lord had encouraged me to remove my name a few months earlier from consideration for becoming the pastor of an amazing church in the Northwest.

I have a vivid memory of looking through the window of the intensive care doors and seeing several physician friends gathered around the attending neurologist. These friends and physicians were offering their counsel as they consulted together and considered various medical options. We received no bills from these good friends. They were just helping their pastor and his family in a time of crisis. Fortunately, the neurologist, who was not from our church, did not take offense. Rather, he remained very open to the input from these fellow physicians.

Miraculously (the neurologist's word), our son awakened from the coma with minimal brain damage. Most of the lost knowledge, which resulted from the trauma to the brain, could be relearned. For example, at the onset of the illness his math abilities as a junior in high school dropped to about third-grade level. During his recuperation, he worked with a tutor who helped him recover most of his former level of abilities. Any remaining brain damaged sites are astonishingly minimal. I thank God for Nate's amazing recovery. I did not know then that with 20/20 hindsight I would one day see its value as a lesson about passing momentum from one person to another and from one ministry to another.

God's Transforming Turning Points

The Sunday morning after Nate's coma, another preacher filled in for me. He preached an amazing sermon on how God redeems the interruptions in life into transformational turning points. This is exactly what happened as a result of this trauma in our family. For instance, I became much more open to praying for miracles. Over the next couple of years God began to move me from private prayers for miraculous healing to public healing services in our mainline church.

It was not an easy transition. How does a pastor of a traditional Presbyterian congregation explore the realm of miraculous healing services without creating confusion and distrust? How do pastors carry the hot coal of private, prayerful guidance from the Holy Spirit into their work as the leader of a congregation? It's all in how we carry the fire.

A few months after our son's miraculous healing became known throughout our community, a retired Pentecostal pastor showed up at our church. He attended worship for several weeks and then made an appointment to introduce himself. At that first meeting in my office, he gave me what he called a prophecy that God was calling me into the healing ministry. He further offered to mentor me in the ministry of miraculous healing. I took him up on his offer, and we spent time over the next few years building enough trust in our relationship that I could receive the hot coal of his healing ministry and bring it into my own congregation.

He specialized in exorcism healings. Although I was not only unfamiliar but also uncomfortable with this arena of healing, I was open. I asked lots of questions, and he explained his theology. We uncovered many theological areas where we agreed to disagree. But we continued our relationship through the disagreements and continued respecting each other's experiences of God as we grew in trust for each other's calling. We clarified together that my healing ministry was dramatically different from his. I learned that I was not called to exorcism but to helping our mainline congregation become a healing community by surrounding hurting people with loving prayers. In addition, I learned that when a congregation is a forgiving community, it releases God to bring emotional and relational healings that sometimes turn into physical healings. As I explored this ministry, the congregation trusted me enough to walk with me into the unknown. We learned to pray for God to heal the roots of bitterness and the wounds of life that may have led to the emergence of a physical illness.

Passing the Fire without Getting Burned

Through slow, trusting relationship building we watched God transport a healing ministry from a retired Pentecostal pastor into our Presbyterian congregation. Transplanting momentum from one ministry to another or from one congregation to another is a very challenging activity, but it is well worth it. How do we pass the fire without someone getting burned?

Have you ever thought about how Abraham and Isaac carried the fire from their camp to the altar where Isaac was to be sacrificed? The Bible tells us that Abraham took two of his servants, the cut wood, and his son Isaac when he set out for the place where God had shown him he should sacrifice his son. On the way Isaac noted that they were carrying the "fire and the wood…" (Gen. 22:7). We know how they carried wood, but how did they carry the fire from the camp to the altar?

We can guess that they were probably carrying an ember or coal. But how did they transport it? Bruce Feiler, in his book *Walking the*

Bible, discovered that Bedouin tribes today continue the ancient tradition of carrying a coal as they break camp and move to the next site. These modern nomads take a hot coal from the fire and place it inside a special non-flammable cane-like plant. They wrap the plant with cotton to hold the heat while it's being transported. When they make camp again, they prepare some tinder, remove the coal from inside the plant, blow on it, and use it to ignite the tinder to start a new fire.[1]

In similar fashion, if we want momentum to spread from one setting to another, we need to treat it like a hot coal being carried to ignite a new fire. Carrying a hot coal of momentum from one ministry to another requires care. What works in one situation seldom can be successfully transplanted directly into another ministry, even within the same congregation. It almost always requires reworking the idea to fit the needs of the new setting. The process is even more difficult when we attempt to transplant momentum from one congregation to another. How do we transport the coal of momentum from a successful ministry to the tinder of a struggling ministry?

Principles of Relational Communication

The key is communication. However, I am not merely talking about the passing on of information but about what I call relational communication. A number of important principles guide relational communication.

Relational communication occurs when there is concern for the person or people receiving the communication.

Is your goal to use people in the service of your own enthusiasm for some project or program? Or is your goal to share your programs because you are convinced the programs will minister to the people? The most common reason an ember goes out in the process of transplanting a fire is that the coal is not safely handed from one person to another. In the process the receiver gets burned. As a result, the receiver feels more used than honored or blessed.

For instance, after being urged to attend a men's retreat, a church member recently responded, "Why should I give my time so that you can reach your goal of two hundred men?" In other words, he felt that the invitation came not out of concern for him but rather out of a zeal to reach the organization's goal. A hot coal must be passed

---

[1]Bruce Feiler, *Walking the Bible: A Journey by Land Through the Five Books of Moses* (New York: Perennial, 2001), 90.

carefully and lovingly. Let's face it. Most of us have been burned sometime in our lives when an overzealous person meant well but unintentionally hurt us. To avoid making the same kind of mistake, we need to make certain that recipients know that the "coal" we are passing to them is intended for their good and is worth receiving.

Relational communication takes time.

It takes time to safely pass the coals, even when your staff and leaders are highly competent. Yes, even experienced leaders find relational communication does not happen overnight. I am blessed by being surrounded by highly motivated, incredibly competent staff and congregational leaders. These leaders not only set high expectations for themselves but also have similar expectations for the rest of their colleagues. One of the amazing people with whom I work is John, the head of our evangelism and communications department. He came to us at midlife from the business world. Having served at high levels in the corporate world, he has little patience for incompetence. His quick mind constantly looks for ways to improve our congregational communication.

I have enjoyed watching John figure out how the church is different from the corporate world of business and finance. It took John a few months to transition from the fast-paced, highly competitive world of sales and marketing in the corporate economy to our world of congregational communications.

John came to us filled with fresh perspectives and immediately recognized opportunities where we could improve our ministries. No one could doubt the goodness of his heart or the potency of his ideas. But he quickly discovered that others on our ministry teams were hesitant to take his suggestions. Fellow ministry leaders seemed to fear being burned by the coals as he tried to hand them off. They were quick to spot the dangers more often than the benefits. Thus, they naturally pulled back when he attempted to hand his coals of enthusiasm to them.

John and I learned together the importance of communicating in such a way that the right people "buy in." This meant that they needed to understand that we were not simply recruiting them for our agenda but sharing ideas that would enhance their ministry. The key was to ask those most affected by any possible changes to help us think through all the aspects of the proposed change. We learned that it takes hours of face-to-face conversations and trust building around the church before others will pick up a hot coal of an idea and help make it successful.

Relational communication is most effective when it is face-to-face.

You have many different ways to communicate a message, including impersonal methods such as e-mails and letters. In face-to-face communication, however, a crucial element comes into play, namely, the nonverbal aspects of communication such as tone of voice and body language. These nonverbal aspects are usually as important, and sometimes even more important, than the actual content of the words.

Unfortunately, modern technology has seduced us into thinking of communication as simply the impersonal transference of ideas. Although this may be the case in certain kinds of communication, relational communication–the kind that spreads momentum–is most likely to be effective when it is face-to-face.

E-mail fails as a relational communication tool.

E-mail is probably the worst possible way to attempt to pass a hot coal. Other impersonal forms of written communication such as announcements in church newsletters and bulletins are nearly as bad. No matter how much we try to sell someone on an exciting new ministry idea, if the relationship is not one of high trust, the other person will usually subvert the passing of the coal. And high trust is built through personal communication.

I am not arguing that e-mail should be abandoned. I use it to good purpose, because in some ways e-mails are helpful. For example, e-mails are useful for setting up meetings or appointments and for confirming the scheduling of appointments. They are helpful for confirming specific data or information. But they are likely to be a miserable failure at anything that requires building high trust in the communication. Don't expect e-mail communications to carry positive momentum. If anything, e-mails tend to escalate problems rather than solve them. This form of communication can actually create negative momentum!

For example, some months ago our early service ran several minutes overtime. This had a direct impact on the parking lots and the following service. We generally do a good job of finishing worship on time so that the departing worshipers free up parking spaces for the next service. On this morning the parking lots got severely snagged and tempers grew short. We had drivers honking at our traffic volunteers. Some worshipers shouted unchristian words. It was ugly. By Monday we were receiving phone complaints from those who drove away in frustration because they couldn't find parking that morning. I needed to address the concerns and clear the air in a staff meeting. No big deal, just a minor bump in the road. Unfortunately, before I had a chance to bring it up at the next staff meeting, one of our staff members tried to address it via e-mail.

The first e-mail from a staff member was fairly innocuous. It went something like this: "Hey, don't forget we have parking problems when the service runs overtime. Please be sensitive to our parking lot needs." In hindsight, we all realize this communication should have been shared conversationally, face-to-face in a staff meeting. Instead, it went out via e-mail. Big mistake! Someone on our worship team responded with a defensive e-mail. Soon we were caught up in a firestorm of critical e-mails. Someone pointed out that worship was a higher priority than the parking lot and that we should not let the tail wag the dog. From there, it escalated quickly. Angry, hurtful e-mails sailed around the office in a matter of hours. Some quoted policies and procedures. Others gave detailed explanations about their particular ministry needs. A staff member, returning from vacation a couple days later, jumped into the fray with an argumentative e-mail that brought up an old issue going back several months. By the end of the week I had to send an e-mail to the entire staff that essentially said, "Stop it! This conversation is over. We will clarify this matter at the next staff meeting."

Because momentum requires trusting communications, e-mail is the wrong way to carry the coals. E-mails are extremely limited and dangerous as a form of communication. If you want to destroy positive momentum and stir up negativity, then send a defensive e-mail.

Relational communication involves personality.

Think about the difference between God sending a personal representative to communicate with us and sending an angel. The angel, like an e-mail message, is much less personal than a prophet. Let's explore why God sent Isaiah instead of an angel to carry a warning to Israel.

Isaiah had a vision of an angel carrying a live coal toward him. "Then one of the seraphs flew to me, holding a live coal that had been taken from the altar with a pair of tongs" (Isa. 6:6). How would you feel if you were Isaiah? He had just confessed his sin: "Woe is me! I am lost, for I am a man of unclean lips, and I live among a people of unclean lips; yet my eyes have seen the King, the LORD of hosts!" (v. 5). Then an angel flew directly at him holding a hot coal taken from the fire at the altar. Wouldn't you be afraid that you were about to be branded for your sins? Even if you deserved it, it still would be terrifying. Yet Isaiah feels safe. He stays still as the angel approaches with the coal. The angel then touches Isaiah's mouth with the burning coal and announces that Isaiah is forgiven and cleansed.

What an amazing act of trust! Personally, I think it would be harder to be Isaiah at the moment the angel approached with the hot coal than to be Abraham taking his son Isaac up the mountain as a sacrifice. Abraham already had shown his trust in God, and this son was his reward. God and Abraham were on good speaking terms. But Isaiah was vulnerable, having just admitted the horror of his sins as well as the hopelessness of his generation. As the angel approached, Isaiah knew he deserved whatever punishment he got. Would his lips be burned beyond repair? Would he ever speak again? The coal cleansed him of his sins. Now, Isaiah was ready to carry the message to those who needed God's forgiveness as well.

Relational communication requires humans, not angels.

I love the moment when God asks, "Whom shall I send, and who will go for us?" (v. 8). Picture the scene. God is on the heavenly throne surrounded by dozens of angels and one human, Isaiah. These angels were God's perfect messengers. Whenever God sent a message through an angel, the message was always correct. God asks, "Whom shall I send?" Can't you see Isaiah gazing around the room and waiting for one of the angels to volunteer? Which angel would take the assignment this time? Then Isaiah realizes that everyone is looking at him! No angels are stepping forward to go. They seem to be waiting for the one human in the place to offer himself. Isaiah realizes what the Lord wants and offers, "Here am I; send me!"

You might ask, Why, if angels were available, would God send a human being? Because, unlike angels, we human beings appreciate the need for tenderness and sensitivity as we carry messages in our world of broken relationships. We carry messages intertwined with our personalities. We not only deliver the message, but we hang around to discuss together the implications of God's message and possibilities for an appropriate response.

Angels, on the other hand, work best when God is delivering a non-negotiable message. "Listen, I need a *yes* or *no* because I have to get back to God and deliver your response," the angel implies. For example, when the angel delivered the message to Mary that she would become pregnant through the Holy Spirit and bear the son of God, was there room for her to negotiate with the angel? Or did the angel expect a clear answer "yes" or "no"? Imagine if Mary had said, "This is a bad time for me. You may not know that Joseph and I are planning a wedding. Listen, I'd love to give myself to God, but how about next year?" Did the angel have authority to negotiate with her? What if Mary had asked questions as to the baby's name? "Jesus? Look Joshua isn't one of my big heroes, so I don't really like naming my son after him. Could we name him Barry?"

Angels are not wired with compassion or negotiation skills. They work well with messages delivered to those who are faithful and ready to respond favorably to God. But what about those messages that need to go to people who are slow to respond or are uncertain in their faith? In Isaiah's day God desired repentance on the part of the people of Israel. The Lord needed a messenger who understood the people's hardness of heart. Isaiah had something no angel has—lips that had been cleansed and a heart that had been forgiven. Isaiah could bring the message in a way no angel could—with compassion. When Isaiah warned of the harsh judgments to come, he could say it with tears in his eyes. In other words, Isaiah understood that the coal that had touched his lips needed to be transported to the people's hearts. Isaiah was authorized not only to speak on God's behalf but also to weep with those who weep and rejoice with those who rejoice. God trusted Isaiah to bear the message through his own personality and vocabulary.

Communications that carry positive momentum require the combination of smiles and tears, body language and tenderness, compassion and trust. Angels and e-mails are ineffective for such communications.

Investing Time in Relationships for Improved Momentum

Relational communication occurs when you get to know one another before sharing your message. This doesn't mean that you have to know everything about one another. That requires a lifetime. But you should know, in particular, something about one another's faith. Each year when we welcome new elders to serve on our board, we hold special classes to instruct them about their responsibilities. Sharing their journeys of faith is an important feature of these classes. Newly-elected elders are asked to tell their stories of how they came into a relationship with Jesus, of times when they have felt far away from or particularly close to God, and of how God is currently at work within them. For that matter, I never start a new ministry team or organize a new committee without spending significant time during the first couple of meetings asking people to introduce themselves and tell their stories of faith. The reason I do this comes out of my own experience.

Twenty years ago, I served on my first denominational level committee—stewardship. The first meeting was scheduled to last for two full days. This meant that committee members would be together for fifteen to twenty hours of work. Many of us had traveled significant distances to attend the meeting. We were all type A personalities—highly driven and very task-oriented. We wanted to use our time effectively and feel a sense of accomplishment by the end of the meeting.

Imagine the shock when the chair of the committee took the first three hours of our time for introductions! He invited each of us to share how we had met Christ and to tell about our journey of faith. As I was inwardly groaning about the waste of time, the chair of the committee explained why these introductions were so important. He said that twenty years from now we would likely not recall a single decision or policy resulting from our two-day meeting, but he was confident that something we heard during these few hours of sharing would stay with us. Indeed, to this day I recall one woman's story of how she came to faith in Christ, but I can't remember a single thing we did during the rest of the meetings.

That committee chair understood something it took me years to appreciate. Every minute invested in getting to know one another is worth hours later when we get into policy debates. It makes a huge difference in the workings of a group when we trust one another and know we are on the same team. If we don't develop a trust for others on the committee, it is likely we will be ineffective in our work. Trust-building activities are worth their weight in gold when it comes to passing the coals of momentum from one person to another and from one ministry to another.

As that Pentecostal pastor and I explored healing ministry, I came to an appreciation for why Jesus sent out his disciples two by two. Although we were very different in our theologies, our mutual trust and friendship helped us appreciate the varieties of ways God's Spirit works. I suspect it takes two to carry the coals of momentum from one ministry to another. It is not enough that one person has zeal and enthusiasm to give away. The "on fire" person needs someone else with the trusting relationships to help pass the excitement on to others. At any rate, it takes relational communications.

CHAPTER 8

Moses' Trumpets Help People Follow the Fiery Cloud

We saw earlier how Hezekiah was able to turn the problem of planning a Passover into a spark of momentum that brought spiritual renewal across his kingdom. Where did he get the idea of holding the Passover a month late? The idea came from Moses. Moses realized that momentum requires not only alignment of the culture to reinforce the direction but also flexibility in specifics. The Passover regulations Moses delivered to the people included a loophole for exceptional circumstances. Certainly, from Hezekiah's perspective, his situation qualified as one of these exceptions.

This loophole resulted from a dilemma that Moses faced during the planning of the second Passover after the Hebrews' departure from Egypt. Some of the men who wanted to participate had accidentally touched a dead body and thereby become ceremonially unclean. They asked Moses what they should do. Moses realized that their inability to participate was dampening their enthusiasm for God, so he asked God for flexibility in the situation. God responded:

> Speak to the Israelites, saying: Anyone of you or your descendants who is unclean through touching a corpse, or is away on a journey, shall still keep the passover to the LORD. In the second month on the fourteenth day... (Num. 9:9–11)

Moses was a master at stirring the dying embers of momentum back into red-hot flames. He knew how to maintain positive momentum in the midst of the challenges of daily life. At first it may appear that Moses had it easier than we do. After all, God clearly guided the Israelites through the wilderness. It was fairly simple to know when to move and when to make camp. Every day a smoky cloud hovered over their holy worship tent, the tabernacle. Every night the cloud gave off a mysterious glow so that it looked like a pillar of fire. Momentum is easy when you have a fiery cloud to follow.

> Whenever the cloud lifted from over the tent, then the Israelites would set out; and in the place where the cloud settled down, there the Israelites would camp. At the command of the LORD the Israelites would set out, and at the command of the LORD they would camp. As long as the cloud rested over the tabernacle, they would remain in camp. Even when the cloud continued over the tabernacle many days, the Israelites would keep the charge of the LORD, and would not set out. Sometimes the cloud would remain a few days over the tabernacle, and according to the command of the LORD they would remain in camp; then according to the command of the LORD they would set out...At the command of the LORD they would camp, and at the command of the LORD they would set out. They kept the charge of the LORD, at the command of the LORD by Moses" (Num. 9:17–20, 23).

Harnessing Momentum

You might be asking, "Who needs momentum when you have such clear signs of God's presence?" Before you take the high road and say, "Not me," consider what happened to the Israelites. When we turn the page of our Bibles to the next chapter, we discover that, even with God's unmistakable direction, they still needed to harness momentum.

The action Moses took to fuel that momentum is described in the tenth chapter of Numbers. God told Moses to develop a trumpet system of communications to organize the people. If the people knew when to settle and when to move, why did they need trumpets to call them together for announcements and specific directions? They needed help so the entire camp of Israelites could line up without getting in one another's way. In addition to calling people together, the trumpet blasts communicated when to go to war and when to celebrate God's blessings. "The LORD spoke to Moses, saying, 'Make two silver trumpets; you shall make them of hammered work; and you shall use them for summoning the congregation, and for breaking camp" (Num. 10:1). The sound of one trumpet meant that only the leaders would gather, but both trumpets together called the whole assembly of Israel. Only priests were allowed to blow these trumpets, lest there be confused signals.

Before we look at how these silver trumpets were used, it's important to understand the difference between the "shofar," the ram's horn, and the silver trumpets ancient Israel used. Although natural horns and silver trumpets were both used for a variety of signals, they had a clear difference in function.

The shofar, ram's horn, symbolized God's voice speaking directly to the people. When God first gave the Ten Commandments to Israel, God's voice was like an extremely loud ram's horn. "As the blast of the trumpet grew louder and louder, Moses would speak and God would answer him in thunder" (Ex. 19:19). The shofar called all the people directly into God's presence for worship.

The silver trumpets, on the other hand, did not symbolize God's direct voice. Moses introduced the silver trumpets to coordinate communication for the camp of Israel. The trumpets were used as a human tool to call various groups together for deliberation and decisions about plans and schedules. The trumpets separated them into groups for accomplishing specific tasks. Often the trumpets separated the leaders from the rest of the people to coordinate specific plans.

A Communications Network Maintains Momentum

The silver trumpets provided a critically needed communications network. They provide an important lesson for us. Churches, like any organization, need coordinated communications for people to move together without getting in one another's way. Here is a simple truth about organizations in general and churches in particular. Momentum requires more than a vision and general direction, even God's vision and direction. It also requires coordination. And the kind of coordination that builds and maintains momentum involves communicating both general goals and specific plans persistently through an established process.

Churches typically make one of two mistakes when it comes to coordinating communications. One is to over-spiritualize things and think that if people stay close to God, everything else will take care of itself. In my experience, this is the tendency in most churches. Congregations tend to not pay enough attention to the importance of their communications.

The other mistake–the opposite of the above–is to rely too completely on carefully coordinated plans and organizational communication without staying close to God. King David made this mistake when he depended entirely on his military background and carefully orchestrated trumpet system to bring him success. When he failed to listen to God's directions, the results were disastrous.

For example, think about David's actions when he decided to bring the ark of God to the city of Jerusalem. Rather than consult the Lord about his plans, David drew on his abilities as a motivational leader and set up a parade. He decided to borrow a technique used by the Philistines to transport their images and idols. Instead of following the traditional means of transport, carrying the ark on the shoulders of the priests, he placed the ark on a cart. The parade instruments featured the silver trumpets used for coordinating the troops (1 Chr. 13:8). In other words, he treated this holy procession as little more than a military parade with religious overtones.

From a human viewpoint, it was a well-coordinated parade. The result, however, was disastrous. The wagon hit a bump, and the ark almost tipped over. When Uzzah touched the ark to stabilize it, he died instantly. Even though the parade looked good, something was desperately wrong at the heart of this activity. It was the equivalent of sounding the trumpets to organize the movement of the camp before God's cloud had moved. Trumpets without the cloud of God's presence create nothing more than a parade without a purpose.

Some churches make the same mistake that David did in this situation. They are well organized and well coordinated, but they're out of step with God. In other words, they have abused the trumpet system. Most churches, however, have yet to appreciate what valuable tools the trumpets can be. Although the trumpets may seem less spiritual than the ram's horn that represents God's voice, they are absolutely necessary for momentum. Coordination does not substitute human efforts for God's directives; rather, it is an effective way for humans to carry out God's directives. Here are some principles about effective coordination to keep in mind.

Principles of Effective Coordination

Coordination requires that we formulate and regularly communicate specific plans for carrying out general goals.

I wish I could simply admonish my congregation with a general goal: Follow the Lord, and everything else will take care of itself. In a perfect world, all that church leaders would have to do is remind the congregation to keep their eyes on Jesus. Just abide near the cloud of God's presence. Let the Holy Spirit's fire guide you. Love the Lord with all your heart, and love your neighbors as yourself. These are wonderful general directions. But most church momentum struggles happen between the cloud of general direction and the trumpet of specific plans. Even after the policies and procedures are agreed on, we still need to persistently communicate both the general directions and the specifics.

Persistent repetition helps us maintain our direction.

Why such persistence? Why keep blowing the trumpet? Because what we regularly think about is like a blaring trumpet that calls us to a specific direction in our lives. The ideas that persist in our minds become self-fulfilling prophecies and develop momentum that takes us in a particular direction. That's why Paul reminded us to think on the things that are true, honorable, just, pure, pleasing, and commendable (Phil. 4:8).

As I write this book, I think back to the very first paper I wrote for a seminary class. It was so poorly written the professor refused to grade it. He handed it back with a note that said I had a nice set of research notes, but now I needed to write the paper. Having majored in the sciences, I had not written many papers through college. Most of my science classes required lab reports, not research papers. My wife, an English major, offered to help teach me to write in graduate school. She had to start with the basics. She could not begin by teaching me to write meaningful paragraphs. We had to start with proper sentences. I doubted that writing was anything I'd ever do very well. Then it happened.

During my last year of seminary I turned in a research paper for a church history class. As the professor handed the papers back, not only did I receive an A for the grade, he suggested that I send the paper to a journal because it was good enough to be published for a broader audience. I was too shocked to respond. The professor had planted a seed in my mind that I began to repeat to myself. "I could write well enough to be published." I repeated this to myself until I believed it, and it became momentum.

What leaders enthusiastically support and persistently communicate leads to organizational momentum.

What we repeat to ourselves leads to personal momentum. The same principle applies to organizations. Some years ago, I was invited to speak at an elders' retreat in a church that was struggling because the members lacked momentum. I shared with this group some of what I had learned in my experience of serving growing churches. I explained my strategy of repeating the central purpose of the church until the people believed it and grew into it. In a previous church I spent my first three years greeting the congregation every Sunday with the words that we were a growing church. The truth was that our net growth that first year was just a few members. Yet I continued announcing confidently the vision God had given me that we were a growing church. By the end of the third year we had added services, outgrown our facilities, and begun planning for a new, expanded sanctuary.

I spent the first three years in my present church greeting the congregation with the first line of a vision statement God gave me after I arrived: "We are a church that believes an encounter with Jesus Christ transforms lives." This statement has dramatically shaped and united our congregational culture around the theme of personal transformation. It is no surprise that Bible study, prayer, and small group involvements have grown dramatically as people seek personal transformation.

As we now move toward a new five-year strategic plan that calls for the expansion of our ministry onto a second campus, we see God calling us not only to enjoy personal transformation through Jesus but also to offer God's blessings to our community. And so I'll soon be revising my Sunday-morning greeting to the congregation to include the transformation of our community by being a blessing to others. Once our leaders have helped refine our vision statement, I'll blow the double trumpets for the whole congregation until we believe it and live it.

Coordination must take place through a well-defined and consistent process.

Coordination must take place through a well-defined and consistent process. Everyone should be aware of the process, and everyone should consistently follow it. Shortly after I arrived in my current church, I realized how disconnected our staff felt. Nearly half the staff was new, and these new people were not yet integrated. Many long-time staff members were floundering as they tried to figure out my leadership style and direction. It was like leading an army with lots of distracting trumpet sounds. Some were moving forward, while others were waiting for clarification. It was not a time of momentum. As one of my associate pastors commented using football imagery, "I'm ready to block for you, but I need to know which way you are running."

It took several months for the staff to learn that I often discuss ideas out loud without making a decision. I like to explore ideas and think out loud. I did not realize that they were taking me more seriously than I intended. As a result, it appeared as though I was giving uncertain trumpet sounds. At first some of our staff assumed that if I said something, then I expected them to follow through and make it happen immediately. I recall having a casual conversation with one of the pastors about a possibility for a new area of ministry. Two weeks later I slipped into the back of the room as he was teaching the church membership class and was astonished to hear him repeat my words as the new direction where our church was headed. Clearly, our system of coordination was still ill-defined.

Uncertain trumpet sounds distract and destroy momentum.

The opportunity for clarifying this system came when I realized that healthy relationships needed to be the central priority of our new direction. Rather than simply tossing this out as my trumpet call, I discussed it at staff meetings for the next few months. We worked together and eventually came up with a phrase that we turned into a momentum motto: "Jesus smiles when we all pull together." Turning it into a trumpet call, we created laminated cards and handed them to all staff members to be put on their desks. There was no doubt now in their minds that this was a direction I wanted us to take.

This became one crucial element of our coordination system: Goals and plans would not come to the staff as directives from me, but would emerge from our joint discussion and decision making. The other crucial element I borrowed from Moses involved using the blare of a single trumpet to gather his leaders together *before* he addressed the entire camp. In a similar way, I make it a point to see that the congregational leaders, including staff and lay leaders, know about and are committed to goals and plans before the congregation is informed.

Leaders need to know some things ahead of the rest of the congregation.

Elected leaders who are left out of the loop wonder if they are nothing more than figureheads expected to rubber stamp decisions that already have been made behind closed doors. When they receive their information via the grapevine, they rightly suspect that someone else is really running the church. The net effects are distrust, unhealthy power struggles, abdication of responsibilities, and slowed momentum. Elected leaders in such churches often find it difficult to enthusiastically support the pastor when they feel left out of the process; instead, they respond passively with a "whatever" attitude.

So the single trumpet calls the leaders first so that they can work with the pastor to clarify and refine plans before announcing them to the whole congregation. When the leaders buy into the vision and participate in making the plans to carry it out, momentum happens.

It's never too late to apologize and clarify.

One night our elders studied Numbers 10 and the importance of the single trumpet calling the leaders before the rest of the congregation. I closed our Bible study time by apologizing to my elders for the times I had sent confusing signals that undercut our momentum as a church. I confessed that I had too often surprised our elders by making public announcements of directions about which I had not told them nor asked for their input. As a result some of them had found themselves in the embarrassing position of being asked to support something that had never been discussed at a board meeting. Following my apology, one of the elders responded that, although he appreciated my enthusiasm and gung ho approach to things, more than once my public announcements had caught him off guard. I certainly had made it more difficult than it needed to be for my board to be supportive as well as to lead.

For instance, when we ran a capital campaign for the expansion of our campus, I made a serious and hurtful communications error. Near the end of the campaign we invited our leaders to make their own financial commitments a few weeks prior to the rest of the congregation. The hope was that we could use the first pledges to spark the momentum of the rest of the congregation. However, the result of these first pledges fell far short of what we had anticipated. So low, in fact, the chair of the capital campaign committee and I decided not to announce the deflated numbers to the campaign committee. Even though the capital campaign committee pushed for full disclosure, we refused to tell them anything, announcing that the total would be held in confidence until the completion of the campaign in a month and then announced to the entire congregation. We thought we were protecting them from bad news.

A few days later we received our first significant commitments (two pledges totaling more than a million dollars). In my excitement, I broke the pledge we had made to the campaign committee. To their surprise I stood before the congregation that very next Sunday, without having run this by anyone, and proudly announced that we already had more than one and a half million dollars in pledges. I thought I was motivating the congregation and building momentum. Although it may have helped a few in the congregation to catch the vision, it injured some of our faithful leaders on the campaign committee. They felt that they had earned the right, as leaders who had invested large amounts of time and energy, to be kept in the loop. They felt betrayed because we had refused to give them answers at the leadership meeting just a few days before. Then I turned around and announced the numbers to the entire congregation. I apologized to them and quickly sought to heal those wounded relationships so that we could celebrate success together by the end of the campaign.

Repairing the Communication Network for Further Momentum

Pastors of churches should never underestimate the value of repairing damaged communication networks, particularly when the church is in the midst of major changes. One year after my *faux pas* with the capital campaign committee, I nearly made the same mistake with my board of elders. Fortunately, my staff leaders reminded me of the power of the single trumpet. We had invested nine months in developing a strategic plan. It had passed through several revisions. Our elders scheduled it for approval in November. As we prepared to present it for the board's approval, the strategic planning committee came up with the idea of illustrating the direction of the plan with a visual image. We asked one of the artists in the church to come up with a drawing of a river flowing from the church out into the desert— the theme of the plan: "From the believers will flow living waters" (see Jn. 7:38). She responded with an amazing pen-and-ink picture that was reproducible for the cover of the strategic plan.

The arrival of this sketch so fired me up that I wanted to use it in my annual address to the congregation in October, scheduled two weeks before the elders would see it. As I rehearsed my speech with my staff leaders, I asked whether I should unveil the new art image to the entire congregation before the elders had seen and approved it. They wisely counseled me to hold off using the art until the elders were in the loop. I followed their advice, and the elders were pleased that I had learned my lesson.

Following a fiery cloud still requires coordination. Because we don't have a fiery cloud hovering over us and guiding us, we need to not only coordinate with our leaders but also communicate specific plans to the whole congregation.

CHAPTER 9

Apostles Cooperate in Their Firestorm Efforts

Several families in our congregation lost their homes during the San Diego firestorm in the fall of 2003. It was one of the strangest Sunday mornings I have ever experienced.

Driving to church early that Sunday, I had noted the strangely colored clouds. I didn't know that a fire was burning on the far side of a nearby mountain. By the time our early service finished, we exited to see brown smoke swirling in clouds past the church. We learned that a fire had burned over the ridge and was raging just a couple miles from the church.

As the second service began, the tension in the sanctuary was obvious. Fearful high school youth huddled prayerfully together to compare notes on whose home might be in the path of the fire. Caring adults embraced the youth with comforting words. We opened the service with prayers for the safety of our families, aware that two families had already lost their homes in the fire. Twice we had to interrupt the service with requests for several people to rush home to help evacuate their families who were in the path of the firestorm.

A number of our volunteers had come to church early that morning not thinking there was any danger, only to learn later that the fire had turned south, putting their homes directly in the line of fire. Our parish nurse, on campus giving flu shots, discovered that her home was threatened and had to leave. A father participating in the Sunday school drama that morning learned that his daughters were evacuating their horses from the corrals and rushed home to help. Many families dressing at home for worship suddenly were forced to grab a few valuables and evacuate quickly. Our parking lot soon became the gathering place where evacuees with children and pets connected with other families whose homes were out of danger.

Over the next few days most of the evacuees were not allowed back into their neighborhoods. Few knew whether or not their homes were lost. Some people regularly called their answering machines, hoping that if the machine picked up it meant their home had been spared. Near the end of the week our families were allowed to return to their neighborhoods. Many were relieved to find their homes intact, but others returned to nothing but a chimney and ashes.

The next Sunday our congregation took up a special offering to provide immediate assistance to our families who were now homeless. The special offerings that morning totaled nearly $80,000. The loving response was incredible! Offers of help poured into the church daily. Talk about momentum! People wanted to help. We had a wonderful sense that as a church we were being the loving people God meant us to be.

We quickly discovered that it was relatively easy for us to be loving and generous. However, directing those generous gifts to the people in need of help was unbelievably complicated. Our leaders discovered it was extremely difficult to trace families who now had neither an address nor a phone. Like the apostles in the early church, we learned that ministry takes more than goodwill and kind intentions. Success breeds momentum only when it is coordinated. This requires the cooperation of the leaders and the entire congregation.

Success Breeds Growing Pains

The early church illustrates the importance of coordination even in the midst of success. Surprisingly, the church's growth increased its conflict. The conflict arose because the church was more than an organization or an emerging institution. It was a movement. With growth, the relationships among the apostles and new converts became complicated by misunderstandings. To keep the movement alive, they needed to do more than simply manage the conflict; they needed to convert it into momentum.

The book of Acts records a conflict situation in the church that directly resulted from its incredible success. The church was growing rapidly and adding new programs as people joined the movement. Not surprisingly, when a group is charting new territory together, misunderstanding and confusion occur. For instance, the exciting ministry of sharing communal meals ran into a snag.

> Now during those days, when the disciples were increasing in number, the Hellenists complained against the Hebrews because their widows were being neglected in the daily distribution of food. And the twelve called together the whole community of the disciples and said, "It is not right that we should neglect the word of God in order to wait on tables. Therefore, friends, select among yourselves seven men of good standing, full of the Spirit and of wisdom, whom we may appoint to this task, while we, for our part, will devote ourselves to prayer and to serving the word." (Acts 6:1–4)

The leaders used this conflict over food distribution to clarify their own callings as well as to distribute the ministry among others. Instead of creating a bottleneck by trying to resolve all the problems themselves, the leaders invited others to become part of the solution by coordinating the ministries of hospitality, compassion, and fellowship. To accomplish more than they had in the past, they seized the opportunity to diversify. Successful diversification requires the coordination of efforts.

I suspect they used the example of Moses as their model for resolving the situation. Moses nearly created a bottleneck in the settling of disputes. As the Israelites traveled through the wilderness, the conflict among them grew to enormous proportions. Moses reached the point where he had no time for prayer or teaching because he was spending all his time settling squabbles between Israelites. "The next day Moses sat as judge for the people, while the people stood around him from morning until evening" (Ex. 18:13). Moses' father-in-law watched the situation and then advised Moses to appoint leaders with the specific gifts needed to handle the task of mediating disputes. When the leaders were appointed, they were to "sit as judges for the people at all times" (v. 22). Only the most difficult cases would be referred to Moses. Jethro explained to Moses that playing to the various gifts of the leaders and delegating responsibility to them would help everyone, including Moses himself.

Empowering Others in the Midst of Growth

One of the defining moments in any emerging movement that is picking up momentum happens when the leaders discover that things are growing beyond their control. Generally what forces such a discovery is the natural conflict that results from growth and change. At that moment, leaders must make one of two choices. Either they can halt the momentum by holding on to their control and limiting the organization to what they can personally manage, or they can empower others to share the leadership for the benefit of the whole group. The first option is easy. The second requires coordination and cooperation.

Years ago, I realized that the momentum of our Arizona church was exploding beyond my control. When I arrived at this church, I inherited a situation in which the pastor did almost everything. He not only ran most of the committee meetings but also kept the minutes and usually wrote the annual reports for the committees. This loving pastor was outstanding (much better than me) in his compassionate caring for widows as well as in making hospital calls. He knew the parishioners by their first names. However, his strength was also his weakness. To give such personal attention and care, he unintentionally limited the congregation to a size that he could manage.

I recall the Sunday morning service when someone asked for an update on one of our members I had not known was in the hospital. I was embarrassed and for a moment felt that I must not be a good pastor. How could one of our members have gone into the hospital without my knowing? I responded that I honestly didn't know about the situation and turned to an elder for more information. I realized that day that I had to choose whether to be the managing pastor who relates caringly with everybody on a first name basis or to give up control and release others to coordinate ministries beyond my abilities. I chose to let the church grow beyond my ability to control it. I'd specialize in preaching and teaching and get out of the way of those whom God was calling to manage various ministries around our church. The same kind of choice inevitably faces all leaders in healthy, growing congregations

I recently visited our local model railroad museum and watched as multiple miniature trains running in different directions shared mostly the same set of tracks. How do trains going in opposite directions and forced to share the same tracks avoid having train wrecks? First, at important places two sets of tracks run parallel, allowing one train to pull out and stop while the other passes. Second, those operating the trains communicate with each other: red and green lights flash, train whistles sound warnings, engineers stay in visual and voice contact with other engineers and rail workers. Both of these steps are crucial because if one train is going to build momentum, other trains must stay safely out of the way.

Coordinating to Avoid Train Wrecks

Most leaders do well at this first step toward momentum. Like train engineers and conductors, these leaders help various groups coordinate their schedules to avoid train wrecks. The various departments may have little in common with each other, just as the purpose and destiny of individual trains have little relationship to one another. Whereas one may be a passenger train, another is simply hauling goods. One train is destined for the West Coast, and the other for the East. Likewise, in most congregations the various groups are little more than a loose confederacy of activities that need to stay out of one another's way.

Coordination can be as simple as maintaining a calendar, holding a monthly board meeting, reporting on the various activities so that others are aware of what each group is doing. "You rehearse your choir on Thursday night, and I'll have my prayer meeting on Tuesday morning." "Who will run off the bulletins next week while Julie is away?" While such coordination is an improvement over the bottleneck created by a leader who insists on controlling every aspect of the organization, it does little to release the momentum that could be gained through cooperation.

Moving from Coordination to Cooperation

Reflect again on the situation in the early church. The apostles had to coordinate their preaching and prayer with the food distribution of the seven leaders who were in charge of the meals. As long as the apostles stayed out of the way of the hospitality team, each group could maintain its own separate momentum. But that was not enough for them to be successful in their larger goal of reaching the world with the transformational message of Jesus. Momentum toward this larger goal required that the apostles move the early church from coordination to cooperation.

Cooperation goes well beyond simply staying out of one another's way. It involves moving from the momentum of separate, individual groups to a synergistic momentum of the whole. Cooperation requires us to unite our efforts in order to accomplish the shared goals of the entire congregation.

During the year of expanding and remodeling our sanctuary, we moved all five of our worship services each weekend to our fellowship hall. This multipurpose room was never intended to house such multiple worship styles. It was no longer enough to coordinate the schedule so that only one group was using it at a time. We regularly needed to move the grand piano to make space for the contemporary singers. We needed to clear space for the children's choir at one service and then make quick changes between services to accommodate our adult choir. The room had to be shifted quickly to fit the differing styles of worship. While our sound people were running microphones and wires from the stage to the choir area, others changed the seating arrangements. Every week the setup was different, depending on which groups were providing the music, drama, or video components. As a result of these multiple shifts, we learned new levels of cooperation.

Cooperation toward shared goals can only happen as people communicate, deal with boundary issues, and learn to trust one another. Coordination can be achieved with minimal communication, but cooperation requires extensive communication with others to receive and give assistance. Boundary issues arise because not everyone will want to cooperate to reach a shared larger goal. You'll hear: "That's my job! Who gave you the authority to do that?" "We've always used that room for our group! Since when do we have to sign up for it?" Communication is essential in resolving these kinds of issues.

Trust is imperative if the communication is to be effective and the boundary issues are to be resolved in a healthy manner. The energy required to build trusting relationships is considerable, but it pays incredible momentum dividends in the long run. Unfortunately, many people who are competent at coordinating multiple individuals and groups do not realize how lack of trust between these same groups and/or individuals limits momentum for the organization as a whole.

Nurturing Trust One Step at a Time

Trusting relationships do not happen automatically; they must be nurtured. Genuine trust is built one step at a time. Those who wish to enjoy the momentum of cooperation must appreciate that trust is always earned.

A member of another church recently approached me for a second opinion on her church's struggles. She was trying to decide how to give some honest feedback (feed-forward) to her pastor. The insight was simple yet profound. She wanted to tell her pastor that the momentum he experienced in his last church did not automatically transfer to his current situation. She was very aware that church members were getting tired of hearing about the wonders of his past congregation. They felt inadequate by comparison. Every time he referred to his last church in glowing terms–"My last congregation was a leader in the community when it came to caring for needy families"–his current congregation shuddered. In fairness, the pastor probably thought he was challenging his congregation to a glowing vision of a shared future. The problem was that he simply assumed he had their trust based on his years of ministry. He didn't realize he hadn't yet earned the trust of his new church and, in fact, was undermining any trust that existed by his invidious comparisons between the present and former congregations.

Years ago, I met with a frustrated Presbyterian deacon who was considering leaving her church. She described how she had been hurt on the night of the deacons board elections. Assuming she was a shoe-in for moderator of the board of deacons, she was caught off guard when someone else was elected in what appeared to be a carefully orchestrated coup. She wondered what she had done wrong. After all, she had already served as the moderator of a deacon board at a much larger church. In fact, in her first year on the board she had often suggested new approaches by prefacing her remarks with the phrase, "At my last church…"

As we talked, she realized that her previous effectiveness was based on relationships nurtured over years. It was naive to believe that those who barely knew her in the new church would automatically have the same level of trust. She had assumed that her previous years of service on another church's deacon board meant she carried trust from that setting to her present church. At first she was frustrated to realize that she needed to earn the trust by slowly building healthy relationships rather than referring to her past accomplishments. But she decided to invest the next year in being a better listener to fellow deacons. Once they saw her servant heart, their attitudes changed. One year after her humiliating defeat, she was elected moderator of the board of deacons.

Building Trusting Relationships

If trust is not automatically granted, how do we build healthy trusting relationships? I once heard Stephen Covey at a San Diego leadership seminar present some helpful insights about earning trust in working relationships. Although I have not found this material in his written works, I have adapted his idea that trust is built one step at a time, like climbing a ladder, for our staff. Here is my version of it.

Ask questions.

At the bottom rung of the ladder, there is practically no trust. At this level, all we have the right to do is ask a question. Questions are not threatening. We simply ask questions to clarify how the other person is thinking. Questions are a way of entering the conversation with humility. For instance, if I'm seeking to clarify my supervisor's thinking, I could ask questions such as, "Why am I sending this memo?" "How is this project related to the event coming up next month?" "Should I send a copy of this to the other deacon in charge of that event?"

Questions allow others to respond and explain their thinking. Only after we have proven ourselves trustworthy through such nonthreatening questions are we ready to take the next step up the ladder of trust.

Make suggestions.

On the second rung of the ladder there is some trust, but not a great deal of it. At this level we can make suggestions. The key to making suggestions in low-trust relationships is to remember that we are not assuming the responsibility to make anything happen. We are simply trying to better understand the organization's culture and to see if our ideas are worth consideration. It's important to avoid pride of ownership and to offer suggestions in a spirit of humility. For example, "I don't know exactly how this works, but maybe our group could consider moving to a different time to free up that room for next week." "This may or may not work, but I was wondering if we could include something else in that mailing." "I don't know if we've tried this before, but perhaps our staff could hold regular monthly meetings intended to build relationships rather than just coordinate our calendars." While decision making remains with those in charge, these suggestions deliver the message that we really want to be helpful.

Offer assistance.

The next rung on the ladder is to increase the trust level of others by not only making suggestions but also offering to assist with their implementation. "I thought it might make everything run more smoothly around here on Tuesdays if we set up the work room before the volunteers arrived. I'd be glad to do it." "How about if we have some refreshments when we meet each week? I could help organize it."

Remember that this is the third rung on the ladder of building trust. Some of the most common boundary misunderstandings occur when a zealous new person jumps to this third rung on the ladder and offers to help without first climbing the lower, nonthreatening rungs of trust. If there is very little trust, such offers of help often are perceived as attempts to usurp another person's authority or take over her job. Instead of promoting teamwork, such offers can feel threatening to the individual or even to the entire group.

Act and report.

When we have earned the trust of others, then we're in a position to do something on their behalf. However, it's also important that we immediately report to them what we have done. "I went ahead and sent that memo in your absence; was that okay?" "I told her you were unavailable and went ahead and answered the question for you." It is important to report immediately so that the person in charge doesn't feel blindsided.

Act on others' behalf.

The final rung on the ladder of trust involves having the confidence to act on behalf of others without needing to report. We're not trying to hide what we have done from the other person or cover what we have done. But we're confident of their trust and do not need to regularly check in on everything we do. We have earned the right to go ahead and act on their behalf.

In our less-than-perfect world, we are constantly going up and down this ladder of trust in all our relationships. When trust is broken, we must start over at the bottom rung. I sometimes remember to use this same trust ladder in my interactions around our home. In one area I may be at the top rung with Kathy. "I went ahead and got the oil changed in your car for the trip next week." In other areas I may be on a lower rung. "Do you kids want to go with us to the concert?"

A Common Enemy Creates Cheap Trust

The easiest and quickest way to build trust and move from coordination to cooperation is to discover a common enemy. When one of the passengers on a hijacked plane over Pennsylvania addressed his fellow passengers with the words "Let's roll!" they had enough information via their cell phones to realize that their hijackers intended to crash that plane. By sharing a common enemy on that morning of September 11, 2001, those passengers gave one another immediate mutual trust to cooperate and accomplish something beyond what one person alone could have done. Their heroic decision to risk their lives in confronting the terrorists involved cooperation and trust.

The early followers of Jesus quickly developed trust when persecution broke out. They found themselves under attack soon after they chose those first seven leaders to distribute food. Stephen, one of the leaders in the hospitality ministry, was put on trial and executed for his belief that Jesus was the Messiah (Acts 7:60). Philip fled from Jerusalem into the neighboring area of Samaria and soon was preaching to people there about his love for Jesus. When several people responded favorably to his message, Peter and John, two of the apostles in Jerusalem, showed their trust in Philip by going to Samaria and blessing what he was doing (Acts 8:14).

Cooperation becomes relatively easy when enemies are trying to destroy our momentum. In the face of crisis, we band together as a trusting team. Our churches are not likely to face the enemy of persecution. But more than one pastor has built trust quickly by rallying the congregation to face a common enemy–the enemy of lost vitality, or lack of direction, or corrupting influences on youth.

Unfortunately, although a common enemy is the quickest and easiest way to build trust, it seldom serves over the long haul as an effective way to maintain that trust. When the battle is over and the enemy no longer unites us, the trust and cooperation we built quickly in the midst of a crisis can fall apart. How can we move beyond temporary moments of cooperation to momentum that will last over the long haul?

CHAPTER 10

Paul Collaborates to Light
a Unity Candle

Does the number of weddings where something went wrong really outnumber the flawless weddings, or is it simply that I more easily recall the mistakes? At a recent wedding the three-year-old flower girl wasn't about to hold hands with the ring bearer. She insisted that the boy's hands were dirty. The flower girl's mother, one of the bride's attendants, was already in place at the front of the sanctuary. So it was all up to the helpless father. He struggled unsuccessfully to get the little girl to take the ring bearer's hand and proceed down the aisle. The girl's pout looked as if it was on the verge of turning into a serious cry. The guests in the huge formal sanctuary turned to see what was causing the commotion and the delay. They'd already watched fourteen bridesmaids and attendants walk solemnly down the long aisle. It was time for action. The flower girl's father quickly picked her up and carried her down the aisle, whispering to her to drop the rose petals. The entire congregation watched the scene with knowing smiles. Then it happened.

As the father got to the middle of the church, the little girl decided she no longer wanted to be carried. Pushing away from her father and leaving him with the basket of flower petals, she ran down the aisle to join the ring bearer (without holding hands of course!). Now the dad was stuck. As everybody burst into laughter, the flower girl's father proceeded slowly down the aisle tossing the flower petals in preparation for the bride.

In my experience, the thing that most often goes amiss at weddings involves the lighting of candles. I've seen mothers driven to tears of frustration as they unsuccessfully tried to light the bride's and groom's candles at the beginning of the ceremony. I've watched a pair of candlelighters so focused on staying coordinated with each other across the aisle that they did not notice a jacket sleeve had caught on fire.

Ironically, the lighting of the unity candle, symbolizing that joining together of two separate lives, wins the prize for causing the most difficulties. I've had outdoor services where the breeze prevented the lighting of the unity candle. I've seen the candle accidentally knocked over. I once had a bride and groom get into a pushing match. He tried to light the unity candle with his candle instead of using the long-handled candlelighter provided, and she tried to shove his dripping candle out of the way. Another time, the bride and groom accidentally blew the smoke from their individual candles directly into my face. I started coughing and wasn't certain I'd be able to finish the wedding.

The Nature of Collaboration

If I've learned anything from these mishaps at weddings, it's the tenuous nature of successful, collaborative action: It is a difficult and challenging task for a group of people to work together to bring about a result they all desire. But if collaboration is a challenge, it is also an imperative. For whether we're talking about a marriage, a family, or an entire congregation, maintaining momentum requires collaboration.

What exactly is collaboration? It requires coordination, but it is more than coordination. It demands cooperation, but it is more than cooperation. Consider what is involved in collaboration. Collaboration requires not only high trust and excellent communication but also an appreciation of diversity. It asks that each individual's activities help move the entire institution–whether a family, a church, or a business–toward its larger goals and overarching purpose. Collaboration demands that individuals coordinate their personal schedules to benefit the whole institution. Collaboration promotes win-win thinking in which individuals want both their own and their colleagues' programs to succeed in order to move the organization forward. Various programs and ministries are not viewed as competitors, but as essential elements in achieving the larger purposes. Instead of individuals going in different directions or protecting their own programs at others' expense, the group focuses on the big picture created by the congregation's vision and purpose.

Collaboration is a dance of partners who are different but want the same results. "Labor" is the root of the word *collaborate*. By adding the prefix co-, meaning "with," we come up with the word *co-labor*, meaning "to work with." A collaborator, thus, is someone who works well with others. He or she is someone who is able to look beyond perceived competitors to team up and work toward a common goal.

The apostle Paul was a collaborator. In his two letters to the Christians in Corinth, we see how he dealt with a situation in which he first had, next lost, then tried to regain the trust necessary for collaborative efforts. When Paul wrote his first letter to the Corinthians, he was clearly operating at a high level of trust with the church members and felt he could be direct about the procedures for taking an offering to help the people of Jerusalem. "Now concerning the collection for the saints: you should follow the directions I gave…" (1 Cor. 16:1).

However, when he referred to this same offering in the second letter, his tone had changed dramatically. Instead of directive language, Paul made humble suggestions. "I do not say this as a command…" (2 Cor. 8:8). "In this matter I am giving my advice…" (2 Cor. 8:10). What had happened to explain this change in tone? Paul had not visited them at the time he had promised. As a result, they felt rejected and hurt. They saw him as their enemy. Yet he reached out to them. "For I wrote you out of much distress and anguish of heart and with many tears, not to cause you pain, but to let you know the abundant love that I have for you" (2 Cor. 2:4).

Paul's concern for collaboration is also evident in the way he reacted to the divisions in the Corinthian church. Look, for example, at the way he responds in the first letter to arguments over whether the Corinthian Christians should follow the teachings of Paul or Apollos. Paul refused to let them think of Apollos as his enemy. He did not see their options as either/or choices. Instead of letting the church think in win/lose categories, Paul pushed them to define his and Apollos's roles as a relationship of collaboration. "We are God's servants, working together" (1 Cor. 3:9). Theirs was a great collaboration. They shared the same goal and purpose: to see the field bring forth a harvest. They were co-laborers with God: Paul planting seeds, Apollos watering the young plants, and God causing them to grow (1 Cor. 3:7).

You could argue that the farming images Paul uses here do not necessarily portray collaborative efforts. Two farm workers can stay out of each other's way and get their separate work done. Although the work of the one who plants must necessarily precede that of the one who waters the young plants, they only need minimal communication with each other. What need is there for collaboration? Where is the dance?

Paul moves us closer to collaboration when he shifts from farming to a construction image. At construction sites the work of two people often depends on each other. Without the foundation, the walls will collapse. Without the roof, the walls are unstable. Each, obviously, needs the other to complete the project. However, are the construction workers really dancing or simply working cooperatively?

Then, as though Paul is struggling to find just the right metaphor, he moves to another image that clearly shows collaboration–the church is like a human body.

> For just as the body is one and has many members, and all the members of the body, though many, are one body, so it is with Christ... Indeed, the body does not consist of one member but of many. If the foot would say, "Because I am not a hand, I do not belong to the body," that would not make it any less a part of the body. And if the ear would say, "Because I am not an eye, I do not belong to the body," that would not make it any less a part of the body. If the whole body were an eye, where would the hearing be? If the whole body were hearing, where would the sense of smell be?...The eye cannot say to the hand, "I have no need of you." Nor again the head to the feet, "I have no need of you"...If one member suffers, all suffer together with it; if one member is honored, all rejoice together with it. (1 Cor. 12:12, 14–17, 21, 26)

This image of the church as a body captures collaboration at its best. Every part of a body depends on the other parts. The movement of one part of the body impacts the rest of the body. The success of the entire body requires all the parts to function together. Each organ functions differently but not independently. Each body part values other parts. Together they take care of one another. For the body to dance, all parts must move together.

A few years ago, my wife and I hiked to the bottom of the Grand Canyon. Kathy argued that I should purchase a pair of good hiking boots, but I fought the idea. I argued that my old boots were still serviceable. I tried them out as we took short hikes up and down nearby mountains in preparation for the big hike. After each short hike I announced: "They're doing just fine. Only one toe hurts a little on the downhill." Kathy insisted that if one toe hurt a little on a three-mile hike, it would be torture by the time we reached the bottom of the Grand Canyon. I finally realized that she was right. Experience has taught me that pain in one small remote part of the body can hold the attention of the rest of the body. So I gave in and bought new boots.

Collaboration Tested

While I was in the Grand Canyon, our staff's capacity for collaboration was severely tested. Just hours before I departed on my grand trek, we learned that our construction schedule was facing last-minute delays. The subcontractors were having difficulty staying out of one another's way in completing the final details. The construction of the organ was conflicting with the completion of the flooring on the platform. To be able to run their highly sensitive computer testing, the sound system engineers needed the construction workers to vacate the building. The net result was that, two weeks before the scheduled date to move in, we realized the new building would not be done.

This delay of the building impacted all of our programs, starting with an entirely new schedule of services. Our youth musical, which takes three months to prepare, needed the new facility at least a week before their performances to rehearse. Our committee planning the dedication services had already contacted government officials and community leaders, as well as scheduled musical groups. The Sunday school leaders had already mailed out several hundred announcements about the new times for two complete Sunday school offerings. We had a crisis on our hands. It was quickly obvious that even the tiniest shift of the schedule affected multiple groups and activities. We needed to find a solution, and I was leaving town.

Before I took off, I assigned our new interim executive pastor to lead a staff meeting to resolve the scheduling conflicts. When one of the staff members asked whether I could take part in the meeting via cell phone, I responded that I would be at the bottom of the Grand Canyon where cell phones don't work. I realized as I left town that this staff meeting was the greatest collaborative test we had faced in my tenure. And I wouldn't be there. All I could do was pray.

However, the meeting turned out to be collaboration at its finest. Refusing to sacrifice any of the ministry programs, the staff worked toward a win-win option that they all could support. The final decision involved everybody having to shift something. The youth musical was moved back to the weekend we had planned for the dedication. The dedication was moved to a later date after the sound system was fully tested. The new worship schedule and Sunday school hours were shifted to the dedication weekend. Some scheduled classes were delayed until the following fall.

The entire staff accepted responsibility for working together to support and communicate the new schedule. Within hours of the meeting, printed announcements went out to those affected by the multiple shifts. By the next weekend, a huge banner across the front of the construction site announced the revised dates for our new worship services and Sunday school classes.

We had been working for years to build high-trust relationships and encourage collaborative work among our staff. On an occasion when we could have collapsed into old competitive attitudes, we remained faithful to Paul's vision that we are to function together like a body. Our interim executive pastor's description of the collaborative energy of that staff meeting was a highlight for me. He noted that our staff not only worked well together through the crisis, but that a warm ambience filled the room. The staff members were enjoying one another. Indeed, one of the benefits of collaboration is that it radiates warmth as well as momentum. Like a dance, the atmosphere of the room included warmth and care for one another.

Dancing between Chaos and Tradition

Crisis and potential conflict were resolved with healthy collaboration. What loomed as chaos turned into a consensual plan for maintaining momentum. Indeed, a group moving with momentum is often a dance between chaos and rigid structure. Only collaboration enables the group to avoid either extreme. The push toward the extremes comes from the differing personalities and abilities of people. Some members of the body are so creative that they are always pressing for change that borders on chaos. Others prefer well-defined structure; but in their efforts to maintain structure, they can lead the organization to become locked in tradition. If the creative members of the organization become overly dominant, everything can become chaotic. Train wrecks are barely avoided, and crises create burnout. On the other hand, if those promoting structure and rules dominate, the organization will tend to harden into deadly policies and procedures that do nothing more than continue the traditions. Healthy organizations develop a renewal cycle by using collaboration to dance between the extremes of chaos and tradition.

As you wend your way between the extremes, it is important to remember that each of them—even though they carry it too far—represents a legitimate need. "For everything there is a season, and a time for every matter under heaven" (Eccl. 3:1). The time spent enforcing rules and coordination helps us avoid train wrecks. The time spent challenging the rules and brainstorming creatively helps us explore out-of-the-box options.

When I arrived at my present church, I found that it was dominated by those with structural and organizational skills. Policies and committees stood on top of procedures and structures. Leaders held meetings to prepare for meetings. Using a corporate approach, the church was structured so that the budget and finances tended to dominate all decisions. Those in the more creative ministries felt that their hands were tied if they wanted to engage in innovation and experimentation. The easy response to new suggestions was that they were not allowed under current policies and procedures or that there was not enough money in the budget.

During my interview for the pastoral position, I asked the business manager whether the mission of the church controlled the money or the money controlled the mission. He paused reflectively and answered honestly that the money basically controlled the mission. Leaders tended to make decisions based on whether money was available rather than on whether a proposal was something important for the church to do.

For my first couple of years here, I encouraged our staff members and leaders to break out of this kind of thinking. I invited our more creative people to dream. I encouraged abundance thinking and risk taking. We explored creative ways of worship and new ministry ideas. I was not surprised when the energy among our more creative people surged as we shifted priorities and found ways to fund some of their dream ministries. The creative people suddenly found our church a fun place to be.

Over the next three years we watched the flames of new ministries dance all around us. When overuse of the buildings and miscommunications between ministries caused near train wrecks, we graciously forgave one another in the spirit of collaboration and promised to work together better in the days ahead. The general atmosphere was one of creativity and exploration, risk and danger. Fast-paced dreaming and expansion had become normative. The phrase our staff developed during that time was "Blessed are the flexible."

One of our music leaders developed his "two-week rule." When it came to worship planning, choir anthems, and music coordination, anything more than two weeks away would likely be changed by the time we printed our Sunday bulletin.

In fact, things were changing so fast around our ministries that a fellow pastor friend, who was vacationing in our area, described to me his experience. He called the church offices on a Friday to find out the times of the Sunday worship services. He was absolutely astonished when the person answering the phone responded, "I'm not sure. Things have been changing so fast around here I had better check to be sure which times we are having now." He told me later that he returned to his own traditional church and challenged his leaders and staff members to imagine what it would be like to have a church culture so open to change that people were no longer sure what time the worship services were held.

Relieving the Anxieties in an Overly Chaotic System

However, although creativity and change energize and promote momentum, they can go too far. They can swirl out of control and become nothing more than chaos. Lack of coordination can become more and more costly as mistakes raise anxiety levels. Wasteful expenditures that could have been avoided frustrate those who are wired to manage carefully and efficiently. How do we know when we have gone too far in the direction of chaos? The system knows. Those gifted with administration will start to battle the chaos by calling for structure.

This happened to us. On a staff retreat some of our more organizationally inclined people shared their discomfort with how disorganized we had become. Staff meetings were inconsistent. Messages and communications were sometimes confusing. Some of our finance staff had wasted way too much time having to trace down paperwork related to expenditures of funds. Lack of coordination was leading to increased stress levels. For them, we were no longer in a collaborative mode. They were trying to survive the disorder that had been thrust upon them. Creativity can be energizing, but chaos is frustrating.

Although the warm and caring ambiance had not vanished, voices were tight and emotions raw as we cleared the air that day. Several staff members asked that we reinstitute a weekly staff meeting to help us better coordinate our schedules and promote our shared vision and goals. Together we clarified the need for additional policies and procedures to guide us. The following Monday, I reinstituted weekly staff meetings.

Our structure people stepped forward to use their gifts and help us create the organizational infrastructure needed to support the creative ministries we had birthed over the previous couple of years. Soon we developed a new handbook of policies and procedures for all employees. We created a strategic plan with some intentional goals for the whole church. We reorganized staffing and committee structures to move us toward the strategic plan. We performed a complete communications audit as well as a congregational survey to determine where we needed to improve to move together toward our intentional goals. Just as the theme of flexibility had dominated our culture for a couple of years, so now structure became the theme for the next season.

As a body with different personalities and gifts, we are learning to dance between chaos and tradition. We appreciate those who are gifted to tweak structures for the organizational support of ministries. We also appreciate those who are creative dreamers and their ability to challenge the rules in order to push the boundaries of our ministries.

Collaboration is the capacity to enjoy and affirm the gifts of others who are different from us. It enables us to both appreciate and maintain the dancing flame of a healthy momentum.

CHAPTER 11

David's Servant-leadership Fans the Flames

Even in Alaska, you have a time to let the woodstove sit empty and cold. During the summer months, when the sun is still shining at midnight, chimneys are cleaned, houses are aired, and neighbors take extra time to visit. Men fell dead trees together and help one another haul and stack the wood in preparation for the next winter. Summer is a time for renewal and a time for a break from the demands of harsh Alaskan winters.

In a similar way, every congregation has seasons when the pace of programs slows. This is part of the normal cycle of growth and is an important time to prepare for future growth. In many congregations, the summer is regularly a slow season. The challenge is how to face up to the waning energy and rev up the momentum when fall rolls around. In other congregations, a slow season occurs when enthusiasm has subsided after some kind of all-church drive or event, when a dissident group has pulled away from the church, when consensus about the church's direction has broken down, when some goal or goals have not been met, and so forth. Slow seasons have several causes. The question is, What should you do when this happens in your congregation?

Responding to Slow Seasons

Most church leaders, initially, use the power vested in their office to get things moving again. Many leaders in crisis automatically turn to a domineering approach to accomplish what they want. Using the authority of their office, they manipulate the congregation through guilt. The pastor stands in the pulpit and announces to the entire congregation: "Our policy states that all parents who use our nursery must volunteer to watch the children one Sunday a month! How can you drop your child off knowing that you haven't served your turn?"

If guilt doesn't work, many try a dose of fear. Consider the pastor embarrassed by the poor turnout for a missionary speaker who filled the pulpit during the pastor's absence. From the pulpit the next week, the preacher lectured the congregation and declared, "I want everyone who missed last week's missionary to stand." Looking angrily at the congregation, he proceeded to harangue the members. "How can you call yourselves Christians? Something must be wrong with your relationship with Jesus if you don't care about the millions of souls going to hell. In fact, I suspect you are in danger of going to hell along with them."

Although these are extreme examples and only a few dysfunctional pastors would use such tactics, most pastors have been tempted to take this kind of approach at some time. Such abuse of power is nothing short of tyranny. And tyranny never creates momentum. Persuasive influence, in contrast, is a very effective tool for generating momentum. Tyranny is efficient (in terms of time and energy demands), but ineffective in the long run and sometimes even in the short run. Influence is less efficient, but effective in the long run and sometimes in the short run as well.

You can see the difference between the two approaches when you compare the leadership styles of King Saul, the tyrant-leader, and King David, the servant-leader. David was a master at managing momentum because he understood both the importance of influence and the means by which he could exert influence, namely, by serving his people. Saul, on the other hand, relied on force to get the people to do what he wanted. Saul's abuse of power not only failed to generate momentum, it killed it. David's servant attitude toward his people built momentum.

Saul's Approach: Tyranny

For example, think of the time when King Saul had grown jealous of David's growing popularity. Saul feared that if David continued to attract followers, when the time came, Saul would be unable to pass his kingdom on to his son, Jonathan. Saul's jealousy grew even greater when he learned that Jonathan not only remained friends with David but also had helped David escape Saul's tyrannical insistence that David be destroyed. Seeing the balance of power shifting, Saul tried to regain his momentum as the king of Israel. He reverted to a fearful display of power.

The story appears in 1 Samuel 22. In his attempt to escape from Saul, David stopped at a village called Nob and requested some bread to continue his journey. A priest there gave David holy bread from the altar; then David continued on his journey. When King Saul learned that a priest at Nob had assisted David's escape, he was furious and decided to make an example of the village. He commanded his troops to kill the entire village. Saul believed he could turn the tide of momentum by imposing his will.

However, King Saul's own troops refused to obey his command to slaughter the priests. The only one willing to obey the command was a foreign mercenary serving in Saul's army. This man, respecting Saul's authority as king, massacred the whole village. Saul had made his point. He had the power to have people killed if they betrayed him or assisted his enemy David. Saul tyrannized villagers everywhere.

Saul did not realize that his decision to punish that village simply sent more people flocking to support David. When the lone survivor of that massacre reported what Saul had done, more people joined David's side against Saul. In fact, the very next chapter describes David saving a neighboring village from the Philistines. What a contrast! David used his power to serve his people and rescue Israelites. Saul misused his power by tyrannizing his people and having Israelites killed.

Power Languages

In their radically different styles, David and Saul spoke different power languages. Saul spoke the language of tyranny, controlling and manipulating people through fear. David spoke the language of service, inviting people to join his team by persuading and empowering them. Tyranny and service are the two most common "power languages."

I am using the idea of "power languages" in the same way we sometimes hear people refer to "love languages." "Love languages" is a paradigm built around the concept that each of us tends to give and receive love in different ways. For instance, my dad loves getting cards and letters. While he enjoys my phone calls and e-mails, he feels more loved through one card in the postbox than lots of e-mails. One of our daughters tends to give and receive love through hugs and physical contact. Ever since she was a little girl, she would cuddle up on a lap and snuggle during a television show. In contrast, one of our sons pretty much avoids physical contact. He feels loved primarily through giving and receiving gifts.

One way to determine a person's primary love languages is to watch how he or she naturally expresses love. We tend to give what we most want. For instance, early in our marriage I learned that Kathy and I have different love languages. During our second year of marriage, with both of us in seminary, I gave Kathy a theology book for her birthday present. She was polite in her appreciation of the gift. I learned that theology books were not as meaningful to her as they were to me. Although it would take me a few years to discern her primary love languages, she quickly knew that one of mine was receiving books.

In this same way, leaders motivate people through the use of various "power languages." Different languages are helpful and useful for various situations. In the terms developed by Ken Blanchard, a leadership mentor, sometimes the leader is a coach, and other times the leader is a director.[1] Sometimes the effective leader stays out of the way, allowing others to be in charge. Sometimes the leader takes control. God empowers us as leaders to use a variety of ways to be helpful to the group. Different styles are needed for differing situations. No one style works all the time.

But in the midst of practicing the skills required to master these legitimate leadership languages, we need to remember the danger of abusing the power languages of manipulation and fear. A wise leader knows that the power language of tyranny is appropriate only in a very few instances. If we are not careful, we can fall into speaking the power languages most often endorsed by the devil—seduction

---

[1]Ken Blanchard, Patricia Zigarmi, and Drea Zigarmi, *Leadership and the One Minute Manager: Increasing Effectiveness through Situational Leadership* (New York: William Morrow, 1985), 47.

and tyranny. Seduction, the offer of pleasures that can never satisfy (pleasures that actually contain hidden destructive elements), is a favorite power language when it comes to the devil's leading an individual astray. But when it comes to leading groups astray, nothing is quite as effective as the devil's power language of tyranny.

Note how the devil tempted Jesus in the wilderness. The evil one respected Jesus so much that he combined seduction with offers of tyrannical power. As leaders, we need to confront our temptations to tyrannize for what they are–the devil's leadership language for groups. The temptations of Jesus, described in Luke 4, teach us what the devil prizes–manipulation and control. In the second temptation, for instance, the devil offered Jesus power over all the kingdoms: "To you I will give their glory and all this authority…" (Lk. 4:6). The devil offered Jesus what the devil enjoyed. Because the devil manipulates and tyrannizes nations, he assumed that Jesus would desire the same thing–to attain world domination.

Jesus rejected this kind of abusive use of power. He had, after all, come to be a servant, not a tyrant. As the apostle Paul said, Jesus did not consider equality with God something to be exploited, but instead he humbled himself by taking the form of a servant (Phil. 2:6–7). Therefore, instead of bringing people into the kingdom by overwhelming them, Jesus chose to lead by wooing people to his cause. His appeal came through the soft caresses of persuasion and influence rather than the heavy hand of coercion. As the perfect servant-leader, Jesus built momentum slowly and patiently. One reason that tyranny is so appealing is that it seems to offer a way to short-circuit the process of growth and quickly achieve the ends we desire. But tyranny is not the way of God, and it is ultimately self-defeating.

Servant-leader versus Tyrant-Leader

Thus, in the church both the tyrant-leader and the servant-leader may want to bring about the same desired and legitimate end result. They may both aim at building up their congregation and making it a spiritually healthy group. The difference is the means used to get to the end. The tyrant tries to force others into compliance. The servant uses respectful, relational approaches to recruit people onto the team in order to accomplish the desired ends. Here are some characteristics of each.

SERVANT-LEADER	TYRANT-LEADER
suggests and encourages	insists
listens before deciding	dictates
edifies others	denigrates others
empowers others	uses others
patient and persistent	impatient
moves slowly toward the goal	wants immediate results
nurtures relationships to accomplish the task	focuses exclusively on the task even at the expense of relationships

Whereas it would be tempting to overly simplify and paint tyranny as always wrong, on occasion a quick command is appropriate. If the firefighter is rescuing a person caught in a burning building, the rescuer doesn't have time explain and win the trust of the victim. Orders are given: "Hold onto my hand!"

Soldiers pinned down in a firefight don't need a leader who is going to slowly explain and woo them to his viewpoint. They want a leader who takes control, gives orders, and makes things happen. Their lives depend on the leader asserting authority and solving the problem quickly. Such control and manipulation are appropriate in some situations.

Manipulation versus Influence

Few congregations are caught in drastic life-and-death situations. The pastor who resorts to tyranny in situations other than absolute emergency, life-or-death crises may succeed in getting quick action, but will lose overall credibility and momentum as a result. When leaders use manipulation instead of influence to maintain their congregation's direction, they set themselves up for unhealthy power battles. Whenever pastors and congregational leaders try to manipulate the congregation to accomplish a project, they play right into the devil's hands. The devil loves power games and turf battles. Why do I refer to the devil as a tyrant? I take my cue from Isaiah.

For Isaiah, the devil was the great illustration of the failure of tyranny. In the midst of his prophecy to the Babylonian king, he described a being that had fallen from heaven. It appears Isaiah was referring to the devil as a rebel angel who refused to obey God. Instead of remaining faithful and humble in God's service, the devil was the angel who wanted to give orders and wield his authority to dominate others (Isa. 14:12–17). Yet he was also the one who fell into terrible judgment. As John Milton noted in *Paradise Lost,* the devil would rather "reign in hell than serve in heaven." Isaiah used the devil's deeds to warn the kings of Babylon about the danger of reverting to tyranny over persuasion. If they were not careful, they would fall into the same trap as the devil. Indeed, his prophecy came true. Nebuchadnezzar, the king of Babylon, stood on the roof of his palace bragging about his accomplishments. "Is this not magnificent Babylon, which I have built as a royal capital by my mighty power and for my glorious majesty?" (Dan. 4:30). Note the egocentric tyrannical language here: "*I* built...by *my* mighty power...for *my* glorious majesty..." Nebuchadnezzar spoke, and the devil smirked and nodded. It isn't surprising that this was spoken just days before Nebuchadnezzar went insane.

The next king of Babylon, Darius, likewise fell into the same temptation of abusing his power. Drunk with his power, Darius decided to show off the temple treasures they had captured from the Jews. As they partied and got drunk with the holy vessels from the Lord's temple, a hand appeared and wrote on the wall that Darius's kingdom was judged and its time was over (Dan. 5). That night, King Darius was killed as the Medes conquered the Babylonians.

Isaiah's warning that absolute power turns a leader into a tyrant rings true throughout world history. Whether it is ancient Babylon or Nazi Germany, empires collapse when their leaders become intoxicated with power. Refusing to respect others, not seeing the value of patiently developing relationships based on winsome influence, tyrants think they can throw their weight around to get what they want. Sadly, the same thing happens in churches.

Years ago, we had a staff member who did not understand the difference between the power languages of tyranny and influence. It showed up in the way he treated fellow staff members. One day he slammed some papers on the desk of an assistant with instructions that he needed copies made immediately. She was busy working on another project at the time. She responded that she was doing some tasks assigned to her by others but would get to his work when she had finished. Then she added that if he needed the copies immediately, he could make the copies himself because nobody was using the copy machine at the time. He angrily leaned over the desk, drawing close to her face, and said, "People like *me* tell people like *you* what to do, and you'll do it!"

Respect Fuels Momentum

The reason that tyranny never builds momentum is because it is essentially disrespectful. Respect fuels the flames of momentum. Without respect, the flame of momentum flickers and dies.

Consider the plight of Jonathan, King Saul's son, who got caught between being loyal to his friend David and honoring his father Saul. On the one hand, his father wanted David dead and the kingdom of Israel to pass to Prince Jonathan. On the other hand, David's growing popularity was gaining momentum, and David trusted his friend to help him survive Saul's hatred. How would Jonathan respond to this battle over his allegiance?

The difference between Jonathan's relationship with his father and his relationship with his friend came down to one thing—respect. His father did not respect him enough to include him in the decisions. Instead, Saul gave commands without Jonathan's knowledge. In one case Jonathan did not know that his father had commanded the entire army to fast until the end of a battle (1 Sam. 14). When Jonathan ate food and his father found out, King Saul was ready to put his own son to death for this infraction. Even though Jonathan knew nothing about the command and had broken it innocently, King Saul was more concerned about his reputation for discipline than his relationship with his son. The troops ransomed Jonathan's life. Saul had the troops' fear, but Jonathan had their love.

King Saul forced Jonathan to make a choice between father and friend. It is easy to appreciate why Jonathan choose friendship over kinship. He chose David because theirs was a relationship of mutual respect. David influenced him because David reasoned with him, dialogued with him, and included him in decisions.

Saul tried to manipulate Jonathan into doing what he wanted done. He controlled information and released it on a need-to-know basis. He would not tell Jonathan his plans regarding David. He thought he could rely entirely on his powerful position as king and father. It doesn't appear that King Saul ever learned that momentum relationships are built on mutual trust and respect as opposed to asserting the power of position to manipulate others.

Respect Earns Trust

David, on the other hand, appreciated the fact that respect earns trust, whereas disrespect destroys trust. For example, David had a chance to kill King Saul in a cave. First Samuel 24 describes how Saul, needing to relieve himself, went alone to a secluded cave. He did not know that David and some of David's men were hiding in that very cave. David's troops encouraged David to simply put an end to the cat-and-mouse game by killing King Saul.

David crawled forward with a knife, but instead of stabbing the vulnerable King, he cut off a small swatch of the robe as Saul performed his business. When King Saul returned to his troops, he heard David call from the cave. Waving the piece of robe, David declared that he could have killed King Saul. Why did David hesitate to boldly murder King Saul? David spared Saul's life to show his respect for God's anointed king.

David realized that killing King Saul would not make him an automatic leader of Israel. If he took Saul's life to gain the formal title but lost the respect of those Israelites close to Saul in the process, he would damage his chances of becoming an effective king for the whole nation. What good would it be to have the official title if he lacked the trust of so many? Instead of exploiting Saul's vulnerability, therefore, David sought to earn the loyalty of the whole nation by showing his respect for the king and proving himself trustworthy. He appreciated that military leadership required more than simply commanding his own troops. For him to be a successful king in Israel, he needed the support of Saul's troops and Saul's supporters as well as the loyalty of his own men.

Respecting Informal Social Structures

David understood something else that is subtler but equally important: The leader must respect not only the people but also the social structures in which they function. In fact, a leader must understand and respect the informal structures of a group as well as the formal organization. David showed this respect when he honored those who were highly regarded in their villages. In effect, this was an affirmation of the informal power structures of the villages.

When I was pastor of that village church in Alaska, I recall learning how important informal structure was and how it significantly impacted the formal organization of the elected officers of the church. It happened when I brought a motion to the elders asking to improve the building by installing a new suspended ceiling in the sanctuary. I told them that, because our oil bills were so staggering in the winter, an insulated ceiling would help the budget. I had done my homework; I knew the square footage to be covered and the cost of the new ceiling. I had even sought a donor from outside the village to assist us. I concluded my remarks and waited for someone to second my motion and begin discussion. Instead, one of the elders moved to adjourn the meeting. Before I knew what had happened, we were heading home. What had I done wrong?

I tried to bring up the idea a second time and received a similar response. Frustrated at congregational dynamics I did not understand, I let it go. Almost a year to the date of my original motion, the same elder who had made the motion to adjourn when I had originally presented my plan (he was the one who generally made the motion to adjourn) stood to his feet near the end of the meeting. In the Tlinget culture, when someone rises to give a speech, it signifies something important. I had no idea what he was going to say. He very solemnly and formally made a motion that we install a new ceiling in the church. He gave the very same reasons I had given a year before. With no discussion, it passed unanimously.

Later I learned what had happened during that intervening year. Because the Tlinget culture is matrilineal (children receive their tribal identification from their mother), the role of women in the culture is very strong. I learned that the men on the board had spent the year discussing the matter with their wives. If the wives agreed to the decision, it would happen. If they disagreed, it would fail. Those who served on the board were the formal leaders. But the formally elected leaders had to make sure their decisions were approved by the informal, but more important, village leaders–the mothers and wives.

As a result of that incident, I have learned to identify the informal as well as the formal structure of my church. I need to know who the opinion leaders are (and they are frequently not among the formal leaders). I need to know what kind of friendship patterns exist (friendships are often more important than anything else in the views held by individuals). I need to know about any animosities that linger from past conflict (sometimes they explain why cooperation between two individuals is difficult to obtain). I need, in other words, to know about those patterns of relating that cannot be portrayed in an organizational chart but are crucial to the way the congregation functions.

In sum, church leaders who want to stimulate congregational momentum must use influence to patiently woo followers to their cause instead of trying to manipulate others to do what they demand. They must show respect for their coworkers and their congregational members, including those with whom they have disagreements. They must honor and work within the informal as well as the formal organization. In all of this, they follow the leadership model of Jesus, who taught us by his words and his deeds to be servant-leaders.

CHAPTER 12

Ahimaaz Promises Heat but Delivers Lukewarmness

James was one of the most lovable students in that year's graduating class. This large Eskimo man in his mid-twenties weighed around three hundred pounds. With English as a second language, he struggled to articulate clearly in his written assignments and class discussions. But the faculty loved him for his big heart and kind spirit. He was the big man on campus who would give the shirt off his back to help others.

James took the role of making the fire in our chapel for the 10:10 p.m. student Bible study. Each Tuesday night I would arrive a few minutes before 10 to find he already had the fire warming the place up nicely. He loved building the fire in the chapel fireplace. It added an ambience to the Bible discussions.

I was not surprised when we announced a weekend tent camping retreat to a neighboring island that James was one of the first students to sign up. He volunteered to be in charge of the fire. He was enthusiastic as we headed out that cloudy day. Friday afternoon as we pitched the tents, made camp, and cooked our first meal, rain began to fall. The rain was the kind of soft sprinkle that the Navajos call "woman rain." By the next day, however, we would awaken to the heavy pounding of "man rain" on the outside of our tents. It came down in buckets. The only source of warmth was our outdoor fire.

James began the day bright-eyed and bushy-tailed. Because the fire had been thoroughly doused by the rain, he enthusiastically began building a fresh fire so we could cook breakfast. When others offered to help, he confidently assured everyone that he knew everything there was to know about building fires and could light a fire anywhere. We watched as raindrops doused match after match before he could ignite the paper and tinder. Then I saw something happen to James. His temper turned sour.

Soon James was shivering, angry, and embarrassed. What had gone wrong? He knew how to make a fire. At least he knew what it took to make a fire in most settings. Although he had the technique down for how to make a fire in the protected chapel on campus or in the dry winter weather on the north slopes of Alaska, he found it difficult to admit that he lacked the skills to make a fire in a wet rainstorm of southeast Alaska.

This cheerful, mild-mannered, gentle giant of a man, forced to face his own less-than-honest assurances, became sullen. Finally, he agreed to let me take over making the fire while he returned to his tent to change into dry clothes and get out of the weather. He hadn't meant to put an egotistical spin to his claims, but had assumed that building a fire in a rainstorm was no different from building fires elsewhere. Unfortunately, he discovered he had injured his own credibility with his fellow students.

Credibility and Momentum

Damaged credibility always costs momentum. Leaders who want to maintain healthy, positive congregational momentum learn to promise less and deliver more. They communicate honestly the expected costs as well as rewards for the congregation to move forward to meet the vision.

How many pastors every year attend seminars in which successful pastors parade their stories of dynamic ministry? While their stories are motivational, the details are worked out in subtleties too numerous to recount. Sadly, not noting the finesse of momentum, inevitably, some good-hearted, well-intentioned pastor heads home filled with dreams of transplanting the ministries of a megachurch in Los Angeles, California, to his struggling congregation of seventy-five in Lizard Tail, Arizona. Then reality sets in.

The pastor comes home with wonderful stories of success, convinced he can copy them. He promises the congregation that their church is destined to be the next megachurch in America. Two years later the pastor, frustrated by failure to fulfill his promises, has lost credibility and momentum and is seeking to move. James's frustration with the fire is the story of many pastors. How can we avoid making this all-too-common momentum mistake?

Transporting Momentum

Ahimaaz knew what James felt that cold rainy day. A minor character in the midst of one of the most tragic stories in the Bible (2 Sam. 15:24–18:33), Ahimaaz was a volunteer runner David recruited to serve as the bearer of news. He carried messages to King David during Israel's civil war when David's son Absalom led an army against his father. Ahimaaz courageously put his life on the line to warn David of dangers. His goal was to help return David to the throne. But he learned that enthusiasm isn't enough to transport momentum from one place to another.

Traditional Preaching Focus

Christian preachers for generations have pointed out how the death of David's rebel son Absalom contains parallels to Jesus' death on the cross. Traditionally, preachers have used the story of Absalom's death to describe insights about Jesus dying on the cross. Like Jesus, Absalom died hanging on a tree suspended between heaven and earth. Like Jesus' spear wound into the heart, Absalom's death involved spears thrust into his heart. In fact, the most significant part of the story, King David's sorrow at the death of his son, reminds Christians of God's deep sorrow at Jesus' death. Tears come to our eyes as we read the anguished cries of David, "Oh my son Absalom, my son, my son Absalom! Would I had died instead of you, O Absalom, my son, my son!" (2 Sam. 18:33). This is a touching description of God's sorrow at the death of Jesus.

This focus on the sorrow of God at the sacrifice of Jesus for our salvation is as far as most preachers take this part of the story of David and Absalom. But when we consider how Ahimaaz carried the message of Absalom's death from the field of battle to King David, then we discover an important momentum lesson. Let's explore with Ahimaaz what it takes to carry a hot coal of momentum from one place to another.

Ahimaaz's Story

Let me summarize Ahimaaz's story. This young man was the son of David's trusted friend, the priest Zadok. David entrusted Ahimaaz and his father to serve as part of a spy team left behind to keep an eye on Absalom's moves when King David and his troops had to abandon Jerusalem. David asked Zadok and Abiathar to remain at Jerusalem serving in their official priestly roles leading worship in the city. Keeping their ears to the ground for any news that might be important to David, these two priests agreed to relay messages to their sons Jonathan and Ahimaaz. These two sons of the priests were the runners to carry the messages from Jerusalem to David.

Jonathan and Ahimaaz were good teammates. They ran together. They hid behind enemy lines together (2 Sam. 17:17–21). They helped David avert a catastrophe when they learned that Absalom was planning to attack David near the river while David's troops were resting.

David's troops, exhausted and feeling defeated as they abandoned Jerusalem, had marched as far as the river. Absalom's army, on the other hand, rode the waves of victory after having just captured the city of Jerusalem. Absalom's troops wanted to use their momentum to pursue David and his men before they had time to recuperate. But the effective warning messages of Ahimaaz and Jonathan allowed David to cross the river in time for his army to escape (2 Sam. 17:22).

Ahimaaz must have been treated like a hero when he helped save the army that day. Delivering important news, he was rewarded with the king's appreciation and attention. King David knew this young man on a first-name basis. What an honor!

So, on the day that David's troops won the civil war against Absalom's troops, it made sense that Ahimaaz wanted to carry the victorious news from the battlefield to David. Ahimaaz arrived on the edge of the celebration just as David's troops gathered around Absalom's dead body. Meanwhile, David waited fearfully back at headquarters for the news. David wanted his troops to defeat his son's army without harming his son. David had given clear instructions to his generals that they not hurt his son. "Deal gently for my sake with the young man Absalom" (2 Sam. 18:5). It was not to be. With his hair caught in a tree, Absalom was killed dangling from the branch.

Joab, the general who stabbed Absalom with a spear, chose a professional runner to carry the message to David. The Cushite runner had no personal investments in the outcome of the civil war. He was simply paid to run messages from the general to the king. David's troops were celebrating their success. The victory meant the momentum had dramatically shifted from Absalom's side to David's. Soon David would return to his palace in Jerusalem. The attempted coup was quelled. Now Joab had to send a runner to deliver this message to David.

The Cushite must have been at Joab's side that day, awaiting his assignment. He saw the whole victory unfold. He watched as Joab finished off Absalom with a spear. Thus, he was sent to the king with a two-part message. David's army was victorious—good news! David's son was dead—sad but necessary. David would not be happy, but he needed to know the truth. Hopefully, in the midst of his sorrow at the truth, David still would catch the momentum of his troops' victory. Joab figured the best way to deliver this news was with minimal emotion. Send the professional runner who had no personal investment in the situation. For the Cushite, it was simply a job.

Ahimaaz's Positive Spin

Ahimaaz, however, begged Joab to let him run also. He wanted to give David the news. Even though Joab already had sent a professional runner to carry the message, Ahimaaz begged that he be allowed to run, too. Joab explained, "You are not to carry tidings today; you may carry tidings another day, but today you shall not do so, because the king's son is dead" (2 Sam. 18:20). However, Ahimaaz continued to beg for the chance to run. Finally, Joab let him run.

Ahimaaz took a short cut through a valley and beat the professional runner to David. But he delivered only a partial message— the exciting part. Panting from his long run, he shouted a victory cry as his greeting. "All is well!" Then, he "prostrated himself before the king with his face to the ground, and said, 'Blessed be the LORD your God, who has delivered up the men who raised their hand against my lord the king'" (2 Sam. 18:28). When David asked the dreaded question about the fate of his son, Ahimaaz sidestepped the question by telling David, "When Joab sent your servant, I saw a great tumult, but I do not know what it was" (2 Sam. 18:29). This half message was ineffective and unsatisfactory as far as David was concerned. It was not until the professional runner arrived that David learned the part of the message he most desired to know but feared to hear, the news that his son had died.

Before we explore what went wrong with Ahimaaz's trying to put a positive spin on the message, notice how the professional runner delivered the news. He saw it as a positive message. When David inquired about Absalom, the professional runner responded, "May the enemies of my lord the king, and all who rise up to do you harm, be like that young man" (2 Sam. 18:32). From his objective professional viewpoint, he was delivering good news; the rebel son was dead.

Ahimaaz knew better. He knew that the king would take the death of his son hard. Ahimaaz hoped he could spread the positive momentum from the battlefield to the king's headquarters by not telling what had happened to Absalom. So Ahimaaz delivered a falsely optimistic message in hopes that it would help. Let's explore why sugarcoating a difficult message hurts rather than helps momentum.

Ignorance or Spin?

Eugene Peterson, in his contemporary language Bible *The Message,* graciously lets Ahimaaz off the hook. Recognizing that the ancient Hebrew text has some uncertainty about the placement of the quotation marks, Peterson suggests that perhaps Ahimaaz did not realize that the king's son was dead. Peterson has Joab saying to Ahimaaz, "You're not the one to deliver the good news today; some other day, maybe, but it's not 'good news' today." Then Peterson places the next sentence in parentheses as though the inspired author is clarifying for the reader what Ahimaaz did not understand: "(This was because the king's son was dead.)."

Did Ahimaaz deliver only the good news because he honestly didn't know that David's son had been killed? Let's explore this possibility. Maybe Ahimaaz simply showed up in time to find the troops celebrating and did not see Absalom's dead body at the center of the celebration. Still, Joab made it clear that the news was not good news. If Ahimaaz did not understand what Joab meant, why didn't he seek clarification from Joab before taking the news to David? Perhaps his error was that he was so excited to run that he took off before he had the whole story.

Momentum Messages Require Truth and Trust

Most congregations can find something here. Well-intentioned people who don't understand the larger context can unintentionally damage their congregation's momentum by carrying unclear partial messages. Momentum messages require truth and trust, not merely good-intentioned versions with optimistic spin. Zeal is not enough when it comes to carrying momentum messages. Full disclosure is better for momentum than partial truths.

I'm thinking of the year we ran several simultaneous Easter services on different parts of our campus. We had traditional worship services in the sanctuary overlapping contemporary worship services in the fellowship hall. I ran from one to the other delivering the same sermon in the various settings.

Our contemporary worship team had planned the fellowship hall services to have an evangelistic conclusion with a specific invitation for people to ask Jesus to be their Lord and Savior. With five hundred in attendance at some of those services and a total of more than one thousand in the fellowship hall over the weekend, we were excited when twenty people responded to the invitation.

Some of our zealous contemporary worshipers couldn't wait to tell their friends in the traditional sanctuary services that the fellowship hall was packed. They wanted to pass the momentum from their side of the campus to the other side. Unfortunately, it was heard differently than intended.

Within a couple weeks we had loyal worshipers of both styles, traditional and contemporary, debating which was the better Easter service. Some overzealous people confused the number of worshipers with the number of new followers of Jesus and concluded that we needed to hire an additional pastor for the hundreds that had come to faith on Easter. Such incorrect and confusing messages temporarily damaged our momentum. The problem with well-intended but partial messages is that they force congregation members to fill in the gaps with faulty assumptions. The result is almost always damaged momentum as church leaders use valuable energy clearing up the misunderstandings.

While I appreciate Eugene Peterson's gracious approach to Ahimaaz, I suspect this young runner knew exactly what he was doing. He had hours of running time to rehearse how he would deliver the message to King David. Like the prodigal son in Jesus' parable ("Father I have sinned against heaven and before you; I am no longer worthy to be called your son..." Lk. 15:18–19), I bet Ahimaaz refined and rehearsed his words as he ran. *"King David, I have good news!"* No. How about this? *"Today is your big day!"* Wait, I have it. *"All is well!"*

Here is what I think happened. Ahimaaz knew that David's son had been killed, but he didn't want to deliver that part of the message. Instead, he attempted to put his own positive spin on the message. He decided to avoid giving the hard part of the message. He wanted credit for the good news, not the bad. "I saw a great tumult, but I do not know what it was."

Spinning Messages Damages Momentum

Ahimaaz, highly invested in David's leadership, thought his spin on the message would help generate positive momentum. This is a common temptation, as our most committed people try to promote momentum by controlling the spin on a message.

The more invested people are in the church, the greater the temptation to control communications in hopes that others will become involved and invested as well. I've had leaders ask me not to announce the giving of a donation for fear that the news might de-motivate the rest of the congregation's giving. "People will stop giving if they hear we received this estate." Others have argued that we should use it with positive spin to increase congregational giving. "Now that we have an estate gift to pay down our debt, you can give directly to your favorite mission project." Unfortunately, in my experience momentum is more often damaged than helped by messages delivered with spin. Intended to motivate others, such messages can damage the leader's credibility.

Remember the story of young George Washington, who refused to tell a lie and courageously faced his punishment for chopping down his father's cherry tree? Most of us have heard this familiar story. There is just one problem. It never happened. In fact, today's historians laugh at the story. It is a classic case of positive spin failing to do what was intended.

In his book *Dare to Be True,* Mark Roberts has a wonderful chapter on rejecting spin.[1] Dr. Roberts invites us to check out the source of that familiar story. It first showed up in a biography of George Washington written by Mason Locke Weems. Weems, a pastor who failed in the parish ministry, developed a career of writing and selling books intended to motivate the youth of America to live with good morals and values. He titled his biography of Washington *A History of the Life and Death, Virtue and Exploits of General George Washington.* In Weems's book we find this famous story of the six-year-old boy who refused to lie to his father. There is no historical evidence of any such event. In fact, given Parson Weems's tendency to creatively add positive spin to many of his stories about Washington, his entire book is highly suspicious.

What irony! Weems intended his book to motivate young people to be truthful, yet it was written with so much spin that today it is laughable. Rather than help his cause, Pastor Weems hurt the cause of truth.

Back to King David and the arrival of the two runners. Imagine how David's heart was broken when nobody delivered to him the

<hr>

[1]Mark D. Roberts, *Dare to Be True* (Colorado Springs: WaterBrook Press, 2003), 45–46.

news of his son's death with compassion and concern. A trusted son of a close friend claimed to know nothing about the fate of his son. In other words, there was so little concern for his son on the field of battle that Ahimaaz hadn't even noticed what had happened to him. The other professional runner arrived and announced it as if it were a positive message of victory. No wonder David sank into a pit of despair and depression. What had been a momentous victory on the field turned into a loss of momentum when the troops saw David's grief.

The Need for Accountability

So how might Ahimaaz have avoided this mistake? The answer goes back to the way he formerly ran his messages to King David. His run the day that Absalom died was different in some very important ways. That day he ran competitively against the other runner instead of running together with him as teammates. Because he failed to see the other runner as a teammate, he missed the opportunity of having a partner hold him accountable for "the whole truth and nothing but the truth."

In the early stories of Ahimaaz as a successful message carrier, he always ran with his friend Jonathan. They most likely encouraged each other as they ran together. Hiding out together, they must have reviewed the messages they were to deliver to David. Having each other as teammates helped them remain faithful. Jonathan was Ahimaaz's accountability partner.

Do you have an accountability partner to challenge your tendency to put a spin on your messages? With the best of intentions most of us add some spin, thinking it will help. This tendency increases the more invested we are in the outcome of the message.

I work with a personal pastoral-leadership coach. He and I check in regularly by phone. A few times a year we spend a full day together. He is my accountability partner when it comes to my being honest with myself as well as with my congregation. He recognizes my tendency to let my congregation off the hook as I try to deliver my messages with positive spin. He knows me well enough to know that I find it difficult to tell the whole truth when I know someone may be hurt by it.

Honestly, it was easier to preach boldly during the first year when I didn't really know the congregation yet. Now that I know the people and love them, it is harder to pierce them with the sword of truth. Now that I am beloved by the congregation, it is tempting to file off the harsh edges of the gospel to make the message more acceptable. I need an accountability partner to keep me faithful to God's truth.

Bill Hybels refers to this difficult task of speaking the truth in love as telling the last ten percent. The first ninety percent is the easy part. We can look for the good. We can compliment and affirm. We celebrate the wonderful things done. But the truth includes honesty about the uncomfortable challenges as well.

When a leader tries to control the message by wrapping it in positive spin, the leader is seen as naïve. In our first capital campaign I was so enthusiastic in all my communications about our impending success that some of our staff members and elders worried that I had no idea what I was doing. "He's a nice guy, but a bit naïve." "Money doesn't grow on trees." "That's easy for him to say, but he doesn't know how we work." In my attempt to remain positive, I put a positive spin on everything. "Of course, our budget is tight because we already have staffed up for future growth" (better to admit that nobody likes struggling with the implications of a tight budget, but if we all sacrifice and pull together, we will make it). "We don't have a parking problem, just a perception problem" (easy to say for the person who isn't out there when the people are honking and shouting unkind things at one another). Many in the congregation remained unconvinced until I showed that I appreciated the difficulties we would have to face together.

Momentum messages must be carried not only with a high level of trust but also with a high level of truth. People need their leaders to be truthful realists as well as optimists. Naïve optimism, displayed by partially true messages bathed in positive spin, more often hurts than helps momentum.

CHAPTER 13

Smoke and Fireweeds

So far, I have offered a variety of concrete actions that can help leaders build and maintain momentum. In these final two chapters, I shift the emphasis from the way you relate to, and work among, your congregation to you yourself. If you are going to carry out the ideas I have discussed, you need to attend to two crucial matters. First, you need to adopt and maintain the mind-set of growth. Second, you need to protect and nurture your physical, emotional, and spiritual health. I'll discuss the latter in the next chapter. Here, we'll look at the mind-set of growth.

The Mind-set of Growth

In Alaska I experienced two seasons of the year: smoke and fireweeds. From September through May, smoke poured from chimneys. From June through August, the fireweeds bloomed. As far as my sinuses were concerned, both were the seasons of sniffles. Let me explain.

I grew up with terrible allergies. When I was still a boy, my parents discovered that cutting the lawn and trimming our oleander hedges caused my eyes to swell nearly shut and set my nose running for hours. By the time I was a teenager, my mother had convinced my dad that I should be excused from yard work and assigned to other chores. In addition, allergy-screening tests revealed that I was particularly sensitive to smoke and pollens and required a weekly regimen of allergy shots.

You can imagine how living in Alaska constantly tested my allergies. Most days smoke from the chimneys dissipated high into the sky. But on other days the smoke hung heavy over the village, and my sinuses complained. For the most part, I survived the smoke of winter in fairly good fashion. However, the summer season of fireweeds was another story. I found the fireweed pollens debilitating— far worse than the chimney smoke. All summer I dosed daily with decongestants.

Many summers in Alaska, I prayed the same question: "Lord, why did you create fireweeds?" I suppose these fast-growing plants, surging to nearly five feet, have a certain beauty. They take over exposed ground and blossom quickly. But for me, they were nothing more than an allergy hassle. So you can imagine my surprise when one day I found myself celebrating the fireweeds as an expression of God's wonderful economy.

It happened a few years after we left Alaska while our family vacationed in Yellowstone National Park. Wildfires had ravaged thousands of acres in the park. We were stunned to see stands of burned tree trunks that reminded us of used matchsticks. After the initial shock we noticed something else—fireweeds. Millions of beautiful blossoming fireweeds blanketed the ground. For the first time I understood why they are called fireweeds. Fireweeds are one of the first plants to emerge through the ashes after a forest fire. Barely has the smoke dissipated when fireweeds start their cycle of growth. They re-clothe the land with vegetation.

A Kingdom of Fecundity

Fireweeds remind us of an important principle of momentum. It is the principle Jesus taught in many of his parables about the kingdom of God—namely, that God's kingdom is a kingdom of fecundity! Fecundity is a nearly forgotten word except for the curse words that have been twisted from it. What a sad commentary that a word so rich in meaning and descriptive of God's kingdom has been twisted into four-letter sexual expletives. I feel sure that most people who use these expletives don't realize the rich, deep roots of the words they are using. Let's claim this word again for Christ!

The dictionary defines fecundity as: "1. The condition of being fertile; fruitfulness; productiveness; fertility...2. The ability, especially in female animals, to produce young in great numbers." Creation reflects the fecundity of its Creator. Our planet displays the fecundity of flora as lush forests, flowering plants, and tasty fruit. God created the animal world so that the smaller herbivorous animals have greater fecundity than the larger predator species. The Easter bunny is a common symbol of fecundity because bunnies breed like–well, like rabbits.

Because our planet is one of incredible fecundity, humans must work to clear the forest to make a place for farming and habitation. "By the sweat of your face you shall eat bread" (Gen. 3:19). In our fecund planet, plants and animals soon reclaim any space not regularly kept clear by human usage. As soon as humans stop using a space, the plants reclaim it, and the animals reinhabit it. Understanding the fecundity of God's world is a key to understanding several of Jesus' momentum parables about the kingdom of God.

Consider the kingdom parables in Matthew 13. These parables assume that life always involves growth and fruitfulness–fecundity. As the crowds following Jesus hit critical mass, Jesus instructed them not to be surprised at the healthy growth of his spiritual movement. "Listen! A sower went out to sow…" (Mt. 13:3). With these words Jesus describes the kingdom of God in the imagery of fecundity.

Fecundity Principles

Growth is normal.

Jesus assumed that seeds naturally grow in fertile soil. In fact, the only way they won't grow is if something stops them from growing. Growth is normal. This is as true with the kingdom of God as it is across our fecund planet. Something is wrong when seeds of the kingdom do not take root and grow. It may be that the devil has attacked the seeds or that distractions have choked the young plants. But these are clear attempts to stop the progress of God's kingdom.

In healthy soil everything grows, even weeds.

The next parable helps to explain that in the kind of world God has created, even that which is opposed to the kingdom will grow. "The kingdom of heaven may be compared to someone who sowed good seed in his field; but while everybody was asleep, an enemy came and sowed weeds among the wheat…" (Mt. 13:24–25). Fertile soil automatically brings growth to whatever is planted. The problem is that an enemy sowed weeds with the wheat.

A weed in one field is a desired plant in another location.

How do we know which are weeds and which are good grain? Jesus instructs his workers to wait until the harvest and then separate the good wheat from the bad weeds. The next verses surprise us as Jesus adds a further parable reflecting that what is considered a weed in one farmer's field may be purposely planted by a neighbor in his garden. Whereas a mustard plant may be nothing more than an irritating weed in a field intended exclusively for wheat, when planted purposely in a garden, the same mustard plant is celebrated as a thing of beauty—an object of appreciation and purpose.

> "The kingdom of heaven is like a mustard seed that someone took and sowed in his field; it is the smallest of all the seeds, but when it has grown it is the greatest of shrubs and becomes a tree, so that the birds of the air come and make nests in its branches." (Mt. 13:31–32)

Alive yeast infiltrates the whole loaf.

As if Jesus hasn't already made the point of God's amazing economy of growth and fecundity, he concludes this section with one more parable. "The kingdom of heaven is like yeast that a woman took and mixed in with three measures of flour until all of it was leavened" (Mt. 13:33). Yeast is even smaller than a mustard seed, yet it is a key ingredient in the final product of the wheat harvest—bread.

A barren plant has a problem.

These parables all assume and declare the same truth: Growth and fruitfulness are a natural part of God's world and the natural outcome in God's kingdom. If the seeds of God's kingdom fail to bring forth fruit, we are to look for an explanation and seek a remedy. That is, if there's no growth, we must correct the problem. In a related parable, Jesus described a fruit tree that was barren. The gardener was given one more chance to fertilize it and make it fruitful. If the last attempt to restore it to health and fruitfulness failed, the tree was to be uprooted to make room for something else to grow (Lk. 13:6–9).

Life Involves Health, Growth, and Reproduction

In God's kingdom, life always involves health, growth, and reproduction. Yet I have run into pastors who maintain that their congregations are vibrant and alive when the churches exhibited few signs of life. I recall listening to a Korean pastor, struggling with English as his second language, as he defended the last seven years of his recent ministry. "I try my best but the people don't like it. They won't listen to what I preach. They leave for other Korean churches." He lowered his head in defeat. His congregation had dwindled to ten people, fifteen on a holiday weekend, while other Korean congregations in the area were thriving. Then he used the classic argument for not changing his ministry style. "God only counts if I am faithful. I don't have to be successful. If there is only one left, I will still do things the same. Even if only one is left, I am faithful."

What do you say to this pastor? Does his remnant theology—we are the faithful few—make Jesus smile? Imagine a gardener using this kind of reasoning in caring for your yard. Picture this:

> You are walking down a street and pass many beautifully manicured well-kept lawns. The landscaping is amazing: trees heavy with fruit, tall and lush hedges, gardens blossoming with incredible roses. And then you come to a house where the yard has clearly been neglected. The trees are scraggly; the lawn is brown; the rose bushes are spotted with fungus and have no blooms. As you take in this bedraggled scene, the gardener comes around the corner of the house. Carrying some trimming tools, he heads into the rose garden. You stop to visit, and the following conversation ensues.
>
> "It looks like you are having some problems with this yard," you comment.
>
> The gardener responds with a smile. "Oh it's just fine. Sometimes plants are just like that."
>
> You look concerned. "Are you sure they are fine? It looks to me as though they aren't getting enough water. Compare these plants with those in the neighbors' yards."
>
> The gardener, now a bit defensive, answers, "That shows how little you know. This lawn and all the plants are on an automatic watering system just like the other homes around here have. Oh sure, this yard may not look like those neighbors' yards, but I maintain this yard the way the landlord wants it. All the landlord asks is that I be faithful."
>
> "Are you sure?" you wonder aloud. "Your yard and trees look as though they are dying, if not dead. Maybe the automatic sprinkler system is broken. Perhaps some fertilizer would help the rose bushes."
>
> Now the gardener begins to shout angrily. "Listen. It's not my yard. I tend this yard for the owner of the house. He left several years ago and told me to take care of the yard

until he returns. The grass and trees were like this when I arrived. My job is not to transform this yard into a lush garden; it's simply to show up each week and keep things the way they were when the owner left."

In exasperation you comment, "Maybe you could talk with the neighbors about how they got their yards looking so nice and see if there's something you could do differently."

"I'm glad you don't own this place," the gardener huffs. "You have no understanding of how difficult this soil is. Your expectations are entirely unreasonable! Now leave me alone; I've got work to do."

Hopefully, your leadership style has little in common with this gardener. Instead of contenting yourself with a declining church or even maintaining the status quo, you want your church to be a healthy and growing part of the kingdom of God. You want your church renewed and to be a part of the "fireweed" revival sweeping the world today.

Yes, revival is occurring throughout the world. Consider, for example, what is happening in China. The ashes left behind when missionaries departed China in the early twentieth century have blossomed into a full-fledged field of fireweed. Conservative estimates indicate that somewhere between 60 and 100 million Christians lived in China by the end of the twentieth century. We have good reason to believe that as many as 28,000 Chinese are encountering Jesus every day. Moreover, Chinese churches are sending missionaries to other parts of the world. These Chinese churches are alive!

Korea is a similar miracle story. The twentieth century dawned with Western missionaries doubting that the Korean culture could be reached with the gospel. In 1900, Korea did not have a single Protestant church. By the end of the century, Seoul (maybe we should think of it as Soul) was home to some of the largest congregations in the world. Today, with one third of the nation Christian, millions of Korean Christians rise before sunrise for prayer meetings. These Korean churches are alive!

The revival has reached Africa as well. Africa was only three percent Christian at the beginning of the twentieth century. By the end of the century, 40 percent of Africans were Christians, with an estimated 25,000 Africans coming to Christ every day. One of the African hotbeds of revival is occurring in Nigeria. Nigerian churches are so excited about what God is doing that they have sent missionaries to Europe. Some churches recently planted by Nigerian missionaries in places such as England and Italy have become the fastest growing churches in Europe. These African churches are alive!

In 1998, Leith Anderson totaled the numbers of conversions happening around the world and realized that 3,000 people were coming to Jesus every hour of every day of every year.[1] This was the same number of converts on the miraculous day of Pentecost described in Acts 2. No wonder Lyle Schaller and other Christian futurists say that the American church of the twenty-first century is headed into a "Fourth Great Awakening."[2]

The Great Awakening in American History

It might help us prepare for this emerging revival by reviewing what happened during the first Great Awakening that swept through the North American colonies in the 1730s. The preacher most involved in this Great Awakening was George Whitfield. His timing and style were exactly right to reach a new breed of Americans.

In his own journals Whitfield described the spread of the American revival by combining images of fire and fecundity. Describing the response to his sermons, he wrote, "...every day I had more and more convincing proof, that a blessed gospel fire had been kindled in the hearts both of ministers and people. At New York, where I preached as usual, I found that the seed sown had sprung up abundantly..."[3]

Benjamin Franklin appreciated the effects of the revival fires sweeping across the colonies. Jumping on board as an entrepreneur, Franklin became Whitfield's publisher and wrote: "Religion is become the subject of most conversation. No books are in request but those of piety."[4] During the years 1739–1741 more than half the books Franklin printed and sold were by or about Whitfield. While Franklin helped make Whitfield famous, Whitfield helped make Franklin wealthy.

The Great Awakening was nothing less than a movement of the Holy Spirit to introduce people to Jesus and set them on fire for God. It particularly attracted those who had shown no previous interest in

---

[1]Leith Anderson, *Leadership that Works* (Minneapolis: Bethany House, 1999), 165–66.

[2]Lyle E. Schaller, "Signs of Hope," in *The Parish Paper,* 530 N. Brainard Street, Naperville, IL 60563-3199, 1998, 1–2.

[3]John Gillies, *Memoirs of Rev. George Whitfield* (Middletown: Hunt and Co., 1841), 106.

[4]Walter Isaacson, *Benjamin Franklin: An American Life* (New York: Simon and Schuster, 2003), 111.

churches because of the perceived irrelevance of most preaching. The awakening touched those who were tired of dogmatic debates about doctrines that did not seem to apply in daily life. George Whitfield proclaimed a simple, nonsectarian Christianity that offered people an experience of God for life here and now. He challenged the familiar denominational loyalties and suggested that the only thing that really counted was the new birth and a vibrant relationship with Jesus.

Whitfield enjoyed dramatizing his supposed conversation with Abraham in heaven. "Father Abraham," he asked, "Are there any Presbyterians in heaven?" The crowds became excited when George Whitfield announced Father Abraham's answer: "No. There are no Presbyterians here in heaven." "What about Quakers?" "No. None of those here." "How about members of the Church of England?" "Nope." Then came the exciting climax that always thrilled the crowds: Those in heaven were simply Christians.

Sadly, while the Holy Spirit swept through the colonies in revival, many church leaders invested most of their energy denouncing Whitfield and defending their traditions. Rather than becoming a part of this exciting movement of God, they defended their dying institutions. We need to think about, and learn from, their response. Ask yourself, How will I respond as the Holy Spirit sweeps through our land in this generation? What if the missionaries arriving from Africa and Asia challenge my traditions and the ways I have typically done church? Would I be open to exploring new ways to grow? How is my church reaching out to a generation allergic to dogma but open to hearing how the Bible stories are relevant to their everyday lives?

Christianity of the Fourth Great Awakening

I've thought long and hard about these questions and anticipate the following. I expect that American Christianity of the Fourth Great Awakening will feel less Western and a little more African, less theological and somewhat more primal. Leaders with cross-cultural experience will be called on to develop an appreciation for the new international Christianity emerging from the global village. Foreign Christianity will surprise many who were active in the twentieth-century American churches because it won't look, smell, taste, or feel like that to which they're accustomed. In fact, its main evangelistic attraction to those outside Christendom will be that it feels so exotic and unfamiliar.

Are we open to new and different ways of expressing our faith? How about such things as Christian tattoos and body piercings? Post-denominational Christianity will very likely include multicultural expressions of music and art, dance and drama. Are we open to these possible directions? Will we be tolerant of differing opinions regarding non-essential doctrines?

Although some will feel threatened, most of you who are reading this book will feel thrilled by the prospects of global revival. Yet the question remains, What can you do to prepare your church leaders and congregation for America's Fourth Great Awakening?

- First, you need to define clearly what life and vitality mean for your congregation.
- Second, the congregational leaders need to live spiritual vitality as well as proclaim it.
- Finally, you need to conduct exit interviews as people leave your church to determine how to keep improving the momentum of your congregation.

Early in my present ministry I clarified my definition of a healthy church. My definition caught many of our leaders by surprise. Most of them had defined spiritual vitality solely by tabulating numbers. If attendance was up, the church was healthy. If giving was up, the church was healthy. If Sunday school or youth group attendance was down, the church was in trouble.

Picking up an image I had heard from a fellow pastor, I suggested we explore the image that our church is a river. Contrasting a river with a lake, I pointed out that the river is moving and active, whereas the lake is passive and still. When you put your boat in the river, it takes you somewhere downstream. The river forces you to move. On the other hand, a boat can sit in one place on a peaceful lake.

Contrasting Success and Vitality

I defined vitality for our church in spiritual terms. There is a difference between success and vitality. Numbers may show success, but they seldom reveal vitality. In fact, using numbers to determine vitality treats the church as little more than a club or business. Social clubs can evaluate success by attendance. Not churches. Businesses look at the bottom line to determine success. Not churches. So what does a vital congregation look like?

I believe a vital church

- should help individuals grow spiritually by nurturing their devotional life and their daily relationship with Jesus.
- should empower laity to experiment with their spiritual gifts in ministries.

- offers a safe place for in-depth discussions of difficult topics.
- encourages its people to engage in relational evangelism with neighbors who don't know Christ.

The overall measurable goal is not numbers, but rather transformed lives and the church's reputation in the community. I told my church leaders that we'd know we were healthy by listening for stories of personal transformation and for stories from the community that we were blessing them.

Becoming a Church of Vital Leaders

After defining the vital church, I had to begin working with the leaders to implement it. What does it look like to take your congregational leaders with you down the river? Take a serious look at your monthly board meetings. Have they become little more than business sessions to enact policy decisions? Sure, you do the perfunctory opening and closing prayers, but are your leaders growing spiritually?

I am convinced that one of the main reasons church leaders feel frustrated as they complete their tour of duty is that they assumed they would grow in their relationship with God by serving their church. Yet most congregational leaders finish their time of service with no spiritual growth. In fact, many become so discouraged after being exposed to the inner politics of the church that they never serve again and even leave the church as they rotate off the board.

This is where I began. I asked our elders whether they had grown spiritually as a result of their recent service on the church board. The answers were consistent. Few felt their service as elders enhanced their relationship with Jesus. No transformed lives here! So we changed our expectations not only for the elders but also for the monthly board meetings. We realized that spiritual growth and personal transformation required time for Bible discussion, prayers, and small groups. The leaders could not ask the congregation to do what they were unwilling to do. As a result, we changed our meetings. The elders voted to go to two meetings a month and devote a significant part of each meeting to Bible study, small group discussion, and prayer. Now when elders rotate off of the board at the end of their three years, I'm happy to report, they comment that their personal spiritual growth was the most valuable part of serving.

Although we shifted the emphasis away from counting numbers as an indication of the spiritual vitality of our congregation, we believed that the number of recent conversions and adult baptisms was an important indicator. Given the fecundity of God's world, in which living things reproduce, I would be concerned if we were not growing in this way. And you should be too.

Pay close attention to how your congregational leaders pray. Are they praying to reproduce? Are they pleading with the Lord that a friend or neighbor will meet Christ? I'm not talking about prayers for more bodies to run committees and do the work. I mean, are your leaders passionate for those who don't know God? If not, why not?

Perhaps your leaders lack confidence in sharing their love for Jesus with those who don't know him. If you don't help them grow in their ability to share their faith, they will expect you to evangelize for them. Churches in which the pastor is seen as the primary evangelist are already dying. They just don't know it yet.

On the other hand, many pastors talk the talk but don't walk the walk when it comes to outreach and personal evangelism. Are you praying for and reaching out to someone who needs Christ? If we pastors are not careful, we can use all our energies running the church and not develop relationships with others in the community. I have met pastors who admit they no longer have a single non-Christian friend.

How are you doing when it comes to personal transformation— becoming more like Christ? Are you gaining fresh insights from the scriptures? Are you stretching your faith and experimenting with new spiritual gift areas to see whether God wants you to do something you haven't done before? When did you last participate in a mission trip that forced you out of your comfort zone so that you had to rely on the Holy Spirit? Isn't that how we grow spiritually?

Finally, do you do exit interviews when people leave your church? Of course, we all lose parishioners through death and relocation. There is nothing we can do about it. Many small churches are located in rural communities where the young move away and leave only the seniors to run the church. But this isn't the case in most of our churches. Many of our people leave because they're unhappy with the church. We can learn a lot if we open ourselves to hear why people are leaving. It may be that they are unhappy about something that could be changed. Perhaps we have not understood their expectations. It takes humility and confidence in God's call to listen when people tell us why they are leaving our church. I know it hurts us when people leave. But if we can learn in the midst of the hurt, isn't it better than repeating our mistakes?

Of course, some people need to leave. If we listen carefully and disagree with their differing vision for our church, it's appropriate to bless them on their way to a church where they can be more supportive. Even that process helps a pastor clarify God's vision and calling for the congregation. If we don't listen but keep doing what we are doing, we will keep getting the results we are getting. If we want different results, we need to learn and change.

Whenever I become discouraged about the state of the church, I go back to Luke 10. I celebrate with Jesus the moment he knew for sure that his movement, though it would have its ups and downs, was picking up momentum. It happened when he heard the report of the seventy disciples he had sent out two by two. Jesus had sent them to prepare the way for him. They were to proclaim healing and peace through the arrival of the kingdom of God and to share in the joyful labor of the harvest. In other words, they were celebrating the fecundity of the kingdom of God (Lk. 10:1–16).

"The seventy returned with joy, saying, 'Lord, in your name even the demons submit to us!' He said to them, 'I watched Satan fall from heaven like a flash of lightning.'" A few moments later, Jesus burst into the smile of a proud parent celebrating the success of a child. "At that same hour Jesus rejoiced in the Holy Spirit..." (Lk. 10:17–21). Jesus celebrated with exuberance! I picture him bursting out in a loud laugh of delight. He knew that his followers were destined to transform the world because they were experiencing the joy of momentum.

We have the opportunity to further the momentum that Jesus set in motion 2,000 years ago. We have amazing opportunities ahead of us. To exploit those opportunities, we must adopt and maintain the mind-set of growth. As we do, we'll make Jesus smile!

CHAPTER 14

Burning the Candle at Both Ends?

It is no coincidence that we use fire imagery to speak of maintaining a desirable direction. When we want to continue the romance in our marriage, we must "keep the spark alive." People in sales must maintain the "fire in their belly" or they lose their competitive edge. Churches pray for God to send "the fires of revival."

Of course, fire imagery can also be used to describe undesirable situations. A "firestorm" is sometimes used to describe a catastrophic situation. "Burning the candle at both ends" is an image of self-destructive behavior.

Candle Flame of Influence

I would like to add another image of fire to the set: Leaders who build and maintain momentum have candle flames of influence burning within them. When leaders quit tending to their personal candle flames of influence, the congregation's zeal for God usually grows cold. But here's a crucial question: To maintain your personal candle flame of influence, do you have to burn the candle at both ends? We all know pastors and other leaders who "burn out" as they desperately try to keep up with the crush of demands and responsibilities. Is that the only way to build and maintain momentum in your church? I say no. In fact, I would argue that both extremes–letting your candle flame die or burning the candle at both ends–are destructive to you and to your church as well.

When I was a freshman in college, one of the first assignments in our chemistry class involved studying the flame of a candle for a half hour. Each student lit a candle and then simply sat and observed the flame, keeping detailed notes. The assignment was intended to heighten our objective observational skills.

At first it seemed like a boring assignment. I wrote the following in my lab book: "The flame burns." "The candle flickers when a door opens and the air shifts." "The flame leaps for a moment and then returns to its regular height." A few minutes into the assignment, I become intrigued with the constant changing of the flame and the candle. The candle was slowly melting and being consumed. I noticed tiny bits of carbon floating in the candle wax near the wick. The carbon pieces swirled in the melted wax, revealing that the wax was in constant subtle motion as it supported the flame. The flame was consuming the wax in a chemical reaction, creating heat and light. The flame was in a dynamic relationship with the subtle airflow of the room.

By the end of the assignment, I realized that a candle flame is all about ongoing subtle but significant changes. The flickering candle flame is a great image for the importance of the personal spiritual life of the leader in building and maintaining momentum. Although a candle flame may not change the temperature of an entire room, it can brighten the immediate space surrounding it. Likewise, church leaders influence their congregations by shining their light.

Candlelight may seem trivial compared to the dramatic images of fire in the Bible. Fire sometimes represents the convulsive events in history that shift the direction of an entire nation or give birth to a new movement. When God called Moses to lead the Israelites out of Egypt, God spoke from a burning bush. Moses' encounter with that fire of God changed history–the nation of Israel was born.

In Acts 2 we read about the followers of Jesus experiencing God's Spirit like flames of fire. "Divided tongues, as of fire, appeared among them, and a tongue rested on each of them" (Acts 2:3). God's presence as fire helped them realize that God was founding something new–the church. The fire of the Holy Spirit came on the whole congregation, not just the apostles. The idea that all of God's people can have the Spirit changed world history.

In the face of such fiery events, of what significance is a leader's small candle flame? Actually, a great deal. For a congregation's momentum is more connected to the daily tending of the individual pastor-leader's candle flame than to the dramatic and miraculous acts of God for the congregation. Without a leader who maintains his or her own flickering candle flame, even congregations who have seen dramatic answers to prayer and miracles will naturally fall back into the familiar, comfortable routines of the past. In fact, as the seven churches in Revelation learned, if pastors do not protect their own candle flame, the churches grow cold and die (Rev. 2–3). Perhaps this is why the Bible reiterates in various stories that the leaders are candles of influence and that the absence of leaders who carefully tend their candle flame is disastrous to the congregation.

Losing the Flame of Momentum

Moses discovered that the flame of momentum could be lost through only forty days of his absence. All he did was leave the people long enough to go up the mountain and receive the Ten Commandments. By the time he returned to the Israelite camp, Moses' spiritual momentum was replaced by Aaron's golden calf.

Nehemiah's influence was a key to the construction of Jerusalem's walls. Although his leadership stirred the people's faith, their momentum flagged on his departure. He was stunned on his return to see how quickly the flames of their enthusiasm for God had been extinguished. They had lost his emphasis on keeping the Sabbath holy. Worship leaders no longer received their salaries. The temple of God had fallen again into benign neglect.

Hezekiah's son failed to continue the spiritual influence of his father, with drastic consequences to the nation. Over and over history repeats for us this same story. Spiritual momentum is wrapped around leaders. Momentum leaders must keep the congregation's vision alive. Without vision the people perish.

Kathy and I hiked last year through some of the western pine forests that are suffering from the attack of bark beetles. It is sad to see how the recent years of drought have weakened the Ponderosa pine trees. They have lost their natural resistance to attack by these beetles. Many western forests that a few years ago were beautiful and lush now display multitudes of standing dead trees.

It is easy to spot a pine tree dying of bark beetles. The tree dies from the top down. At first the tree may still look healthy and fine. But the top branches are already brown. Once the top of the tree turns brown, it is too late to save the tree. After the bark beetles have laid their eggs, thousands of larvae eat their way under the bark. They eventually emerge as adult beetles, boring holes through the bark to attack the next tree. Coming across the fully dead carcass of such a tree displays not only bark riddled with thousands of holes but also wood with interwoven trails left by the larvae.

Congregations, like pine trees attacked by bark beetles, die from the top down. It may take a congregation several years to play out the dying process, but once the pastor and congregational leaders have lost their passion for God's call, momentum quickly fades. New leaders and/or a new pastor are usually the only hope to reignite the fires of momentum. Otherwise, the congregation naturally sinks into purely maintenance activities that are nothing more than a slow dying process.

Recognizing the Problem

I am astonished how many congregational leaders define a dying church as acceptable. Is this God's will? Where is the God of fecundity who created our incredible planet with its burgeoning life? God has created our world so that life involves growth and reproduction. All healthy flora and fauna both grow and reproduce themselves. How, then, can a church leader argue that a congregation is healthy and alive if it is failing to reproduce and is losing members?

Some pastors defend their declining congregation as the blessed remnant. A congregation that is not reproducing by passing the faith onto others is affirmed as spiritually healthy. A church that has lost momentum is said to be doing just fine. Sadly, often these leaders do not even recognize the problem.

No wonder Timothy, a young pastor of the early church, was instructed to "rekindle the gift of God that is within you" (2 Tim. 1:6). In other words, momentum requires leaders to nurture their personal flames of influence. When a pastor's flame dies, whether from burnout or any other cause, the church begins to die as well.

Tragically, the destructive consequences for a church when the leader's flame dies out may continue even when a pastor finally leaves and the church begins the process of getting a new pastor. A dying church–a church without vision and unified direction–will devolve into an organization with factions that advocate differing visions of what the church should be. Some will simply want to maintain the status quo. Some will claim that renewal will come when everyone in the church is doctrinally pure. Some will argue for a focus on youth as a way to revive the congregation. Some will look to a particular kind of new pastor as the only hope. Having different images of what the church should be and how the dying process can be reversed, the factions engage in a culture war. Each faction tries to spark its own momentum as it strives to move the congregation in a different direction from that advocated by other factions.

Of course, the factions do not acknowledge the nature of the conflict. They do not define it as a culture war. But in my experience, no matter how strongly Christians try to pretend that their fights are about theology, doctrine, absolute truth, or any other "noble" cause, in reality most church fights are really culture wars, a struggle over which vision of the church's direction will prevail.

Even the arrival of a new pastor won't immediately end the fighting. Minor, and sometimes major, skirmishes over the congregational direction can continue. For example, picture the following situation. The new pastor wants to control the various committees more than the former pastor. Some conservatives in the congregation see this as a step in the right direction, believing that the old pastor was too loose on some important issues and that it is time for the church to tighten its standards of membership, speak out on important moral issues, and push tithing. Thus, those who welcome these changes warmly support the new pastor.

The loyal opposition, who loved the former pastor, watch things change for a few months. As they grow increasingly uncomfortable with what is happening, phrases such as "It doesn't feel like my church anymore" and "I don't feel fed when the new pastor preaches" begin to swirl around the church. Informal, parking-lot meetings turn into complaint sessions as the loyal supporters of the former pastor ask friends if they have noticed how unloving and unwelcoming their new pastor is. Eventually, they may organize a letter campaign to the lay leaders of the congregation. Or a group may confront the new pastor, assuring him that they are speaking for "lots of people who won't come talk to you."

As the conflict heats up, both groups describe the issues in theological terms. For one side it is about reaching out to share God's love with our neighbors. The other side is defending the doctrines of orthodox Christianity. Usually, neither side realizes that it is essentially a culture war that has no right or wrong. The real issue is whose vision of the church is going to prevail. Eventually, those who win enough battles along the way will determine which culture their congregation adopts. Losers may leave, and winners generally stay. Everything settles down until the congregation fights its next culture war.

Minimizing Culture Wars

How do we minimize such culture wars in our congregations? The best way to avoid church fights is for pastors and congregational leaders to tend their own candle flames and to avoid burnout. Healthy leaders–those who tend to their physical, emotional, and spiritual health–lead healthy churches. The longer a healthy pastor serves a congregation, the healthier the local church will be. Show me a church with spiritual momentum sparked by healthy leaders, and I'll show you a church that is unlikely to deteriorate into factional culture wars.

Pastors who understand and maintain momentum for their vision, then, also give their churches the blessing of minimizing the potential for culture wars. A long-term, popular pastor can sometimes do this entirely through personality and charisma. The better way for the pastor to help the congregation avoid a future culture war is to articulate a clear strategic direction that establishes and reinforces an intentional congregational culture.

Tending Your Personal Candle of Momentum

So how does the pastor tend the personal candle of momentum? It comes to the basics we all know but find so easy to forget–personal devotion, accountability, proper care of body and emotions, and honesty about limitations.

To be a momentum pastor, then, you must maintain a regular devotional life. We recently had a sad farewell at the conclusion of our interim executive pastor's service with us. For the vast majority of people, the one thing he most impressed on them was his phrase, "Seven for seven." Bill taught our new members, our staff, and our elders that lives are transformed when we spend devotional time in the scriptures seven days a week. Often during his two-year tenure he would stop one of us on the staff and ask, "Are you seven for seven?" Many of our people have grown spiritually to new depths simply by maintaining this personal discipline.

How many pastors practice the discipline of spending time with the Lord every day? I am not talking about time for sermon preparation. I am not referring to time in preparing a Bible study class you teach. I mean an intimate time of simply listening to God speak to your heart. How are you doing at letting God love you?

My friend Alan, pastor at Hollywood Presbyterian, led our staff retreat in 2004. He told us about one of his seminary professors who always left parties by ten o'clock in the evening. On his exit from a party this professor would comment to the students, "I have an early morning appointment." Years later, Alan learned that the appointment was this professor's devotional time with Jesus.

Pastors can have the best sermons in the world. They can lead incredibly insightful Bible study classes. They can visit and pray and lead meetings and run the church. But without tending the candle of a personal relationship with Jesus, the tree begins to die at the top.

You must also tend to your physical and emotional well-being and learn to live within your limitations. I realized this two years ago when, after twenty-three years in ministry, I almost quit. Like most pastors, I mentally resign when I get extremely frustrated, but this situation was different. My wife knew I was so serious about resigning before Thanksgiving that she insisted I not do anything radical or reactionary until after the holidays.

Here is what happened. I let myself become so worn out and frustrated that I gave in to depression. From the outside, others figured I was doing great. The church was in the midst of healthy growth. We had wonderful worship services in our newly expanded facilities. The major capital expansion had gone well. But I was not tending my candle flame. My schedule had deteriorated into constant running from crisis to crisis. In the new growth, I had taken too much on myself. Now I wanted out.

When I met with a psychiatrist friend and explained my situation, he asked if I had suicidal thoughts. I commented that I would never take my life, but I often wished it were over. I wanted to have a huge boulder accidentally fall on me while my wife and I were out hiking in the forest. I wanted to not wake up in the morning. He explained that these thoughts represented a passive form of suicidal thinking. It was time for me to make some major changes.

Over the next few months I went on medication, dieted to lose some weight, started an exercise regime, and hired a pastoral coach to work with me. I recall my first meeting with the pastoral coach. I explained that I needed to leave the pressures of the job. The church was too large; too many people were expecting too much of me; I wasn't wired for this kind of stress... My coach responded calmly, "Bruce, nobody is wired for the way you are currently doing your ministry. Now, let's figure out a different way to do it."

Within months I had reclaimed my schedule and returned to a regular healthy balance of feeding my own soul through study and prayer. The creative juices were flowing again. I was laughing at home and waking up after a full night's sleep, energized and excited to be serving the Lord.

Staying Accountable

Pastor, are you tending your candle flame? Are you keeping yourself as spiritually, physically, and emotionally fit as you can? This question brings up the crucial issue of accountability. Have you established a relationship or a covenant group that holds you accountable for keeping your candle burning? Do you have a confession partner who knows your secret struggles with temptation? Who checks in with you to be sure you are being faithful with God's gifts? In other words, who pastors you, pastor?

I have a missionary friend in Africa who sadly proclaims that the number one cause of missionaries failing on the field is their inability to get along with fellow Christians. These good-hearted servants of Christ, by not maintaining personal accountability, become lone rangers for Jesus. Without accountability, it is easy to lose momentum and perspective.

Although they overlap to some extent, I have different accountability partners for different parts of my life. One holds me accountable for my need to keep my family a priority because I constantly battle my tendency to be a workaholic. "Bruce, have you taken time with Kathy lately? Are you taking your day off? How are the kids doing? What are your vacation plans with the family? What is the latest news about that grandchild?" Another prayer partner checks in to make sure I am faithfully maintaining my personal study time to stay mentally and spiritually healthy. "Are you keeping one day a week to read and study?" I purposely surround myself with covenant partners and prayer partners who check in with me to keep me faithful to the Lord's call.

Note: Spouses make wonderful lovers and friends, but may not make good accountability partners. If your issue is weight, I do not suggest you ask your spouse to become your accountability partner. If you are tempted to overspend your budget, it will add stress to your marriage to expect your spouse to help keep you in check. For those who struggle with lust, I don't encourage you to invite your spouse into the battle of the mind where you struggle to take every thought captive for Christ. Seek out accountability partners and covenantal groups that can bring some objectivity.

Accountability helps us change in the positive ways we want to grow. For instance, you will soon finish reading this book. By reading this book, you have shown that you want to become a better leader for your congregation. But if all you do is read this book and put it down, nothing will change. You need to create accountability not only for your personal well-being but also for your ministry as a momentum leader. Here is how it works.

Being Accountable as a Momentum Leader

Begin by clarifying what it is you need to change. Are there one or two skills you have learned in this book that you want to develop to become a better momentum leader? Pause right now and ask the Lord, "What are the one or two things I should start working on to become a more effective leader?" As soon as you finish reading this chapter, flip back through this book and find the ideas you want to implement. Earmark the pages. Next, write in the margins of the page the skills you will need and how you will develop them so that you can use the ideas in your own work. Also, write a name of a possible accountability partner to help you develop a plan for change.

Then, create an accountability system by securing and sharing with your partner what you want to do. Explain to him or her your understanding of the skills needed to implement the ideas and the benefits they would bring to your congregation. Ask for feed-forward about how you could develop the skills. Then ask them to check back with you regularly to see how you are doing at practicing the new skills and implementing the ideas.

Pastor, you need these accountability relationships.

Finally, you pastors need to remember that you are servants of Jesus, not the saviors of your congregations. Unlike the miraculous bush that burned without being consumed, ordinary fire consumes fuel. As I watched that candle flame in college chemistry class, I realized that the wick was not really burning. Rather, it was feeding the candle wax to the fire as fuel. The wick was helping the rest of the candle perform its function. Pastor, you are the wick of your congregation, not the wax.

Momentum pastors tend their own flames by helping their congregations fulfill their God-given purpose. Once I started learning to tend my own flame more carefully and started becoming healthy, I determined that God wanted me to stay in the ministry. I'll never forget the comment of a congregation member and midlife seminary student as she affirmed me for my progress at showing balance and being a better servant-leader. She commented, "Bruce, watching you explode in self-immolation would have brought no glory to God and would not have been good for the congregation."

Pastor, there is no reason for you to burn the candle at both ends in self-sacrifice. Jesus already died for the church, so you don't have to. Let's learn to be momentum leaders who serve our people by staying healthy ourselves, by empowering them for the work of ministry, and by helping them discover the joy of being part of a dynamic congregation.

Careers without College

Heating-and-Air-Conditioning Servicer

by Susan Clinton

Content Consultant:
Robert L. Shepherd
Technical Director
Plumbing-Heating-Cooling-Contractors-
National Association

C A P S T O N E
H IGH /L OW B OOKS
an imprint of Capstone Press

C A P S T O N E　　P R E S S
818 North Willow Street • Mankato, Minnesota 56001
http://www.capstone-press.com

Library of Congress Cataloging-in-Publication Data
Clinton, Susan.
　　Heating-and-air conditioning servicer / by Susan Clinton.
　　　　p.cm.--(Careers without college)
　　Includes bibliographical references (p. 42) and index.
　　Summary: Outlines the educational requirements, duties, salary, employment
outlook, and possible future positions of heating-and-air conditioning servicers.
　　ISBN 1-56065-703-0
　　1. Heating--Equipment and supplies--Maintenance and repair--Vocational
guidance. 2. Air conditioning--Equipment and supplies--Maintenance and repair--
Vocational guidance. [1. Heating—Equipment and supplies—Maintenance and
repair--Vocational guidance. 2. Air conditioning--Equipment and supplies--
Maintenance and repair--Vocational guidance. 3. Vocational guidance.]
I. Title. II. Series: Careers without college (Mankato, Minn.)
TH7015.C55 1998
697'.00028'8--DC21　　　　　　　　　　　　　　　　　　97-35226
　　　　　　　　　　　　　　　　　　　　　　　　　　　　CIP
　　　　　　　　　　　　　　　　　　　　　　　　　　　　AC

Photo Credits:
Jack Glisson, 17, 28
Steve C. Healey, 12, 20, 44
Maguire PhotograFX/Joe Maguire, cover, 11, 22, 25, 30
The News, 43
Photo Network/Eric R. Berndt, 37; Mike Moreland, 14
Phillip Roullard, 4, 32
James L. Shaffer, 6, 27, 34, 47
Unicorn Stock Photos/Eric R. Berndt, 18; Rod Furgason, 39; Martin R. Jon, 9

Table of Contents

Fast Facts

Career Title	Heating-and-Air-Conditioning Servicer
Minimum Educational Requirement	High school diploma
Certification Requirement	None
U.S. Salary Range	$15,000 to $42,000
Canadian Salary Range	$15,000 to $53,900 (Canadian dollars)
U.S. Job Outlook	Faster than the average
Canadian Job Outlook	Faster than the average
DOT Cluster (Dictionary of Occupational Titles)	Machine trades occupations
DOT Number	637.261-014
GOE Number (Guide for Occupational Exploration)	05.05.09
NOC (National Occupational Classification—Canada)	7313

Job Responsibilities

Heating-and-air-conditioning (HAC) servicers design systems that heat and cool buildings. They also put in and set up machines that heat and cool buildings. Heating systems keep buildings warm inside during winter. Air-conditioning systems keep them cool during summer. HAC systems help people live and work in comfort and safety. Another name for HAC servicers is heating-ventilating-and-air-conditioning (HVAC) servicers.

HAC servicers put in and set up machines that heat and cool buildings.

7

HAC servicers fix heating and cooling equipment. They check the equipment regularly to be sure everything is working properly.

Climate

Heating-and-air-conditioning systems make the air inside buildings different from the air outside. They control climate. Climate is the temperature, humidity, and quality of the air. Temperature is the degree of heat in something. Humidity is a measure of the moisture in the air. The systems also filter out dust and odors.

Some equipment that people and businesses use requires exact climate control. Too much humidity or dust in the air can cause equipment to break down. Servicers install special machines to protect this equipment.

Kinds of Servicers

HAC servicers work on systems for houses, malls, hospitals, and buses. They also work on systems for airplanes, factories, and

HAC servicers work on systems for houses.

8

movie theaters. HAC servicers also fix systems in automobiles.

HAC servicers usually specialize in one type of work. Some servicers design new systems. Other HAC servicers sell systems and equipment. Some are installers. Installers put in and set up equipment. Others maintain and repair HAC systems. Maintain means to keep in good working condition.

Many servicers specialize in one kind of equipment. Some air-conditioning servicers install large air-conditioning systems for entire factories or skyscrapers. Others install and service small window-unit air-conditioners in homes.

Furnace servicers install, maintain, and repair heating units. Some servicers work with only one kind of system. Oil-burner mechanics work with systems that burn oil. Gas-burner mechanics work with systems that burn natural gas. These servicers may also work with gas-powered appliances such as stoves or clothes dryers.

Furnace servicers install, maintain, and repair heating units.

What the Job Is Like

HAC servicers may have to work in unpleasant conditions. Broken systems may cause buildings to become very cold or very hot. Servicers installing systems in new buildings often work outside. Servicers may work on skyscraper roofs or in small spaces. Leaky systems and faulty electric wires can be dangerous. Some system components are big and heavy. These can be hard to move into place.

HAC servicers may have to work in small spaces.

Skills

HAC servicers need certain skills. They must know how heating-and air-conditioning systems work. They must know how to test systems to find problems. Then they need to know how to fix the systems.

HAC servicers must be able to read blueprints. Blueprints are detailed drawings that show how all the parts of a system fit together. HAC servicers must follow blueprints exactly. They must put all parts together correctly. Blueprints show HAC servicers where wires and ducts connect. A duct is a tube that carries air or liquid from place to place. HAC servicers must make sure wires and ducts connect at the right places. HAC servicers also check blueprints to fix broken systems.

HAC servicers must be skilled at working with tools. They use hand tools such as hammers, wrenches, pliers, and screwdrivers. They also use power tools such as drills and pipe cutters. HAC servicers use welding torches to connect pipes and

HAC servicers must be skilled at working with tools.

ducts. Weld means to join two pieces of metal together by heating them until they melt.

HAC servicers must understand how machines and electrical parts work. Cooling and heating systems have motors, pumps, fans, and compressors. A compressor is a machine that presses something so it fits into a small space. Compressors work like pumps. They put pressure on gases or liquids to push them through pipes.

HAC servicers must know what each part of a system does to install or fix it. Heating-and-air-conditioning systems have condensers. Condensers change gases into liquids. Heating and cooling systems also use thermostats. Thermostats control the temperature of air in heating-and-air-conditioning systems.

HAC servicers know how to test each part of a system. Servicers test new systems to make sure each part works. They find and replace broken parts.

HAC servicers know how to test each part of a system.

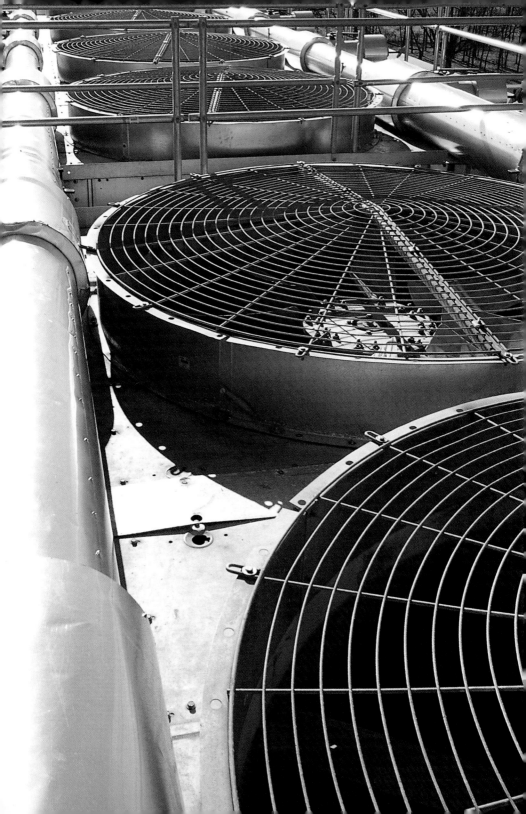

HAC servicers make regular service calls to check systems and keep them working. They test all parts of the systems. They use different kinds of meters to read the results. Meters are machines that measure quantities of gases or electricity.

Where HAC Servicers Work

More than half of all HAC servicers work for heating and cooling contractors. A contractor is a businessperson who does building work for clients. A client is a customer. HAC contractors hire servicers to install and service heating and cooling systems.

Some jobs involve putting together big systems on construction sites. Some jobs involve making repair calls to local homes and businesses. Some HAC servicers make many calls in one day. Other servicers may work on one big job for a long time.

Utility companies hire heating and cooling servicers to call on their customers. These HAC servicers check on customers' heating and cooling equipment. They make sure the equipment works well.

Some jobs involve putting together big systems on construction sites.

Sales

Some HAC servicers sell systems and services. They call future clients. They ask if clients need them for upcoming jobs. This is an important job. Without sales work, jobs would be hard to find.

Servicers who do sales work must also keep up with new ideas in the field. They write reports about their work. Servicers who work for equipment dealers also do sales work. Equipment dealers sell machines to contractors and HAC servicers.

Some servicers work for manufacturers of heating-and-air-conditioning equipment. These servicers help plan, build, and test new products. They work with engineers. Engineers plan and build new machines or structures.

Some HAC servicers go into business for themselves. They become contractors or consultants. They may become equipment dealers, sales workers, or installers.

Some HAC servicers go into business for themselves.

Chapter 3

Training

Many high school classes help students prepare for careers as HAC servicers. Shop or vocational classes teach students how to use hand tools, power tools, and welding equipment. Classes in mechanical drawing are also helpful. Blueprints are a kind of mechanical drawing. Classes in electrical mechanics teach students about motors and heating-and-cooling systems.

HAC servicers work with measurements to install systems.

Math classes are also helpful. HAC servicers work with measurements to install systems. They use math formulas to decide if systems will work well. They figure energy costs of systems. Courses in physics and chemistry are useful for these tasks. Many heating-and-air-conditioning systems include computers. Classes in computers and computer software are helpful.

Touring the shops of contractors or the factories of equipment manufacturers is also helpful. Students should talk to HAC servicers about their jobs. Magazines for air-conditioning, refrigeration and heating servicers are good places to find advice. Students should read these magazines to better understand the field.

Supervised Training

People who have graduated from high school can work in assistant positions. An assistant is a person who learns on the job. Assistants do simple tasks. Experienced HAC servicers

Experienced HAC servicers supervise assistants.

supervise them. Assistants learn more difficult parts of the job as they work.

Many employers prefer hiring applicants who have training beyond high school. Some people receive training through apprenticeships. An apprentice is someone who learns by working with a skilled person. Unions often sponsor apprenticeship programs. A union is a group that seeks better treatment and fair pay for workers.

Apprentices must have high school diplomas. They must also pass tests to get formal apprenticeships. Apprenticeships may last 3 or 4 years. Workers are qualified HAC servicers when they finish their apprenticeships.

Many associations and technical and vocational schools also offer training programs in heating and air-conditioning. Some programs last one year. Others take up to four years. Students learn about all the components of heating-and-air-conditioning systems. They also learn how to install systems and find problems.

Workers are qualified HAC servicers when they finish their apprenticeships.

Servicers learn how to fix systems and how to test them.

Getting Certification

Workers need special licenses or certificates to get jobs as HAC servicers. Some organizations offer certification. Certification is official recognition of a person's abilities and skills.

HAC servicers who work with air-conditioning systems must get special certificates. The gases that air-conditioning systems use to cool air can be dangerous. Servicers cannot let the gases escape into the air. They must pump the gases into tanks. HAC servicers receive certificates when they pass tests.

HAC servicers who work with air-conditioning systems must get special certificates.

Chapter 4

Salary and Job Outlook

The number of jobs for HAC servicers will grow in coming years. New buildings need new heating and cooling systems. Older systems need repair.

Earnings

Earnings for HAC servicers vary. Different types of employers pay different amounts of money. Apprentices usually receive less pay than trained

Apprentices may earn as much as beginning servicers by the end of their apprenticeships.

servicers. But they may get raises during the apprenticeship. Apprentices may earn as much as beginning servicers by the end of their apprenticeships. Beginning servicers with an associate's degree earn about $15,000 per year.

Experienced servicers earn more. Average yearly pay is between $23,400 and $26,000. But some servicers make much more than that. Servicers can earn $42,000 or more per year.

Many HAC servicers work 40 hours per week. Servicers work more hours in some seasons. Air-conditioning servicers may have many calls during summer. Heating servicers are busiest during winter.

Many employers offer health insurance, paid vacations, and pension plans in addition to yearly pay. Health insurance is protection from the costs of getting sick. People pay small amounts to insurance companies each month. The insurance companies pay most of the bills if people become sick. Pensions are salaries paid to people who no longer work.

Air-conditioning servicers may have many calls during summer.

33

Chapter 5

Where the Job Can Lead

There are many ways for HAC servicers to advance. Most advance by improving their skills and knowledge. Some servicers specialize in certain types or brands of equipment. They may become experts in more complicated systems or in servicing certain customers' systems.

Some HAC servicers specialize in certain types or brands of equipment.

Many servicers take training courses. These courses help them keep up with new equipment and methods. HAC servicers who have training are valuable to their employers.

Advancement

Some HAC servicers can become supervisors. A supervisor is a person who oversees the work of other workers. They direct other servicers. They have to keep track of all the work on a large project. They may come in to help other servicers on difficult problems.

Some servicers move into sales. HAC servicers learn all about different products. Their knowledge and experience helps them become good salespeople. Servicers working for manufacturers may sell equipment to dealers or customers. Servicers working for contractors may also act as salespeople. Servicers who work in sales usually make more money.

Some HAC servicers may open their own installation services.

Some servicers go into business for themselves. They may open their own installation services, contractor's businesses, or dealerships.

HAC servicers who understand different kinds of equipment usually get the best jobs. They also have good chances for steady pay raises. Keeping up with changes in the field makes servicers good employees. HAC servicers have many possible career paths and ways to succeed.

HAC servicers who understand different kinds of equipment usually get the best jobs.

Words to Know

apprentice (uh-PREN-tiss)—someone who learns by working with a skilled person

blueprint (BLOO-print)—detailed drawings that show how all the parts of a system fit together

climate (KLYE-mit)—the temperature, humidity, and quality of the air

compressor (kuhm-PRESS-ur)—a machine that presses something so it fits into a small space

contractor (KON-trakt-ur)—a businessperson who does building work for clients

duct (DUHKT)—a tube that carries air or liquid from place to place

health insurance (HELTH in-SHU-ruhnss)—protection from the costs of getting sick

humidity (hyoo-MIH-du-tee)—the measure of the moisture in the air

installer (in-STAWL-er)—workers who put in and set up equipment

maintain (mayn-TAYN)—to keep in good working condition

supervisor (SOO-pur-vye-zur)—a person who oversees the work of other workers

temperature (TEM-pur-uh-chur)—the degree of heat in something

thermostat (THUR-muh-stat)—a device that controls the temperature of the air in heating and cooling systems

union (YOON-yuhn)—a group that seeks better treatment and fair pay for workers

weld (WELD)—to join two pieces of metal together by heating them until they melt

To Learn More

Budzik, Richard. *Opportunities in Heating, Ventilation, Air Conditioning, and Refrigeration Careers*. Lincolnwood, Ill.: VGM Career Books, 1996.

Lytle, Elizabeth Stewart. *Careers in Plumbing, Heating, and Cooling*. New York: Rosen Group, 1995.

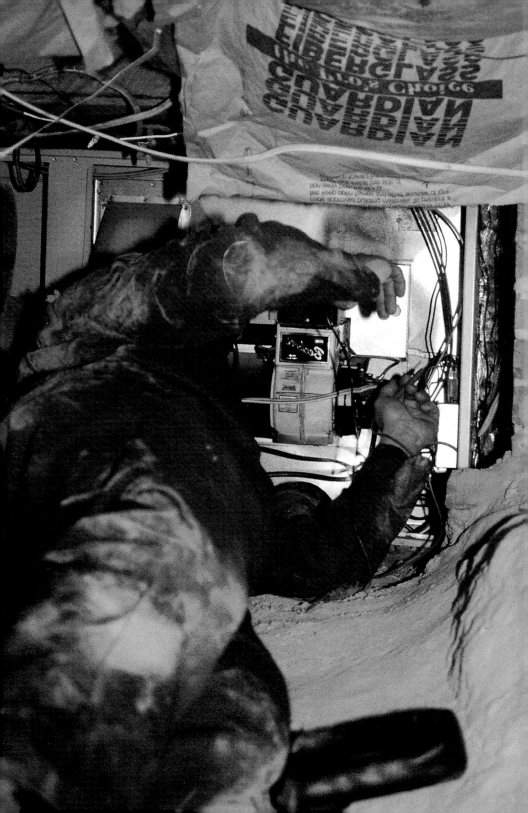

Useful
Addresses

Air Conditioning Contractors of America
1712 New Hampshire Avenue NW
Washington, DC 20009

**American Society of Heating, Refrigerating
and Air-Conditioning Engineers**
1791 Tullie Circle NE
Atlanta, GA 30329

**Plumbing-Heating-Cooling-Contractors-
National Association**
PO Box 6808
180 South Washington Street
Falls Church, VA 22040

Internet Sites

Heating, Air-Conditioning, and Refrigeration Technicians
http://stats.bls.gov/oco/ocos192.htm

HVAC City
http://www.hvac-city.com/

Plumbing-Heating-Cooling-Contractors-National Association
http://www.naphcc.org

San Antonio Conditioning Contractors Association
http://www.acca-saacca.org/

Index